Why is it Wrong to Whine and Complain?

Spying is scary - how could I be a brave spy?

how coln I make God happy?

To

Lee

From

Jell Breseue

Date

MOSES

Takes a Road Trip

And Other Famous Journeys

MOSES

JILL & STUART BRISCOE
pictures and cartoons by **RUSS FLINT**
music by **LARRY MOORE**

Baker Books

A Division of Baker Book House Co
Grand Rapids, Michigan 49516

Takes a Road Trip

And Other Famous Journeys

Text copyright 1996 by Jill and Stuart Briscoe
Music copyright 1996 by Larry Moore
Art copyright 1996 by Russ Flint

Published by Baker Books
a division of Baker Book House Company
P.O. Box 6287, Grand Rapids, MI 49516-6287

Printed in the United States of America

Library of Congress Cataloging-in-Publication Data

Briscoe, Jill.
    Moses takes a road trip : and other famous journeys ; book 1 / Jill and Stuart Briscoe ; Russ Flint, illustrator.
        p.   cm.
    ISBN 0–8010-4183-X
    1. Bible stories, English—O.T. I. Briscoe, D. Stuart.
II. Flint, Russ. III. Title.
BS551.2.B74   1996
221.9'505—dc20   94-36790

An accompanying tape (ISBN 0–8010-3017-X) is available from the publisher. It features a children's group singing all the songs in the four books and the Briscoes reading selections from the "Let's Pretend" and "Let's Make a Video" sections.

This book is produced in cooperation with Alive Communications, Inc., 1465 Kelly Johnson Blvd., Suite 320, Colorado Springs, CO 80920.

CONTENTS

100742

To
our grandchildren
whom we love so dearly

May this book
bring delight to your hearts
and more love
and appreciation
for the God whom we serve.

We gratefully appreciate the following people who made this project a delight.

Betty De Vries, a wise and skillful editor, whose vision for a children's book coincided with ours and whose skill far exceeded our abilities.

Kappie Griesell, who so diligently dug out the Neat Facts.

Larry Moore, who took our words and added his delightful music that sets our feet tapping and our hearts singing.

Russ Flint, whose art is so entrancing and interesting that we wonder if anyone will read our text.

There's something special about this book

 To

catch by surprise
and to surprise with joy
freshen
and excite new attention
in the old, old story

 To

peek around the corner of a verse
and delight to see
who is coming

 To

smell the smells
admire the rich clothes
and glimpse the colors
of worlds different from ours

 To

break the bread of life
into small enough pieces
for young minds
to thoroughly digest

 To

tell of Jesus—
from Genesis to Revelation

 To

discover truths old and new
young and old
child and adult
together

 To

experience
with laughter and tears
simple retelling of old stories
allowing imagination
to refresh favorite events
using songs and simple dramas
to promote understanding

To

know God better
love God more

To

share these discoveries
with a lost, hurting world
of children
and adults

To

this end
authors
artist
composer
publisher

invite you to enjoy
Book 1, *Moses Takes
a Road Trip: And Other
Famous Journeys*!

Letter to Parents

Now that our three children are in their "thirty somethings," we realize we have been parents an aggregate of over a hundred years.

There's more!

As our children have produced nine grandchildren, at last count, we have accumulated almost forty years of grandparenting.

So you could say we have a vested interest in children.

We enjoy telling stories to youngsters, answering their questions, hearing them laugh, and watching their eyes light up with understanding. There's nothing quite like a fire, a cozy chair, a child, an adult, and a good children's book.

"Read us a story, Papa Stu," elicits a special response, especially when I have a good story available.

"Tell us about Daniel and the lions, Grandma," will energize even a fatigued senior citizen.

With these things in mind, we started to work on this project. We wanted to produce something that would convey the old, old story in a new and fresh way. Our intention was that children, long familiar with Bible stories, would be drawn to them once again because they were presented differently. How differently? Well, we are firm believers in children having their own imaginative capabilities and their special brand of humor. So "straight stories" are immediately followed by imaginative, humorous "Let's Pretend" tales.

Parents may be surprised to learn that Jonah's whale was called Wally and that the seagulls observing his watery excursion were called Beagull and Deegull, and that mountains talk to giraffes, but children will take it in their stride. And they'll love Russ Flint's pictures and cartoons and funny little sketches. They'll laugh and so will you.

Our primary aim is to lead young children and adults alike to a wider knowledge of the Book of Books. May you find these books interesting, endearing, entertaining, educational, and inspiring.

Happy reading,

Jill and Stuart

The first five books of the Bible have long names: Genesis, Exodus, Leviticus, Numbers, and Deuteronomy. Most Christians believe they were written by Moses.

Genesis means "beginnings." It tells how the world began when God made it and everything in it, including people. Everything was beautiful when God made it, and Adam and Eve were very happy. One day they did what God did not want them to do. That was the beginning of sin.

Everything started to go wrong. God decided to send his Son to put things right. He would be born into a family just like any other boy or girl.

God chose Abram to begin his family. Abram and his wife had many problems, but they trusted God through them all. As the years passed, their family became quite big. The family leader was Jacob, whose name God changed to Israel.

Exodus means "a way out." Israel had gone to live in Egypt. His family had been there for many years and had become very large and was called the children of Israel or Israelites. The Egyptians were very mean to the Israelites. God decided to show them "the way out" of Egypt.

Pharaoh, the Egyptian king, did not want to let the children of Israel go. So God worked miracles through Moses, the great leader of the Israelites. The Israelites escaped from Egypt into the wilderness, but life was very difficult there. Again God helped them and showed that he loved them. He wanted them to love him in return and to live in a way that showed him their love.

THE BOOKS OF THE

Leviticus is about some of the Israelites called Levites. When the people did some bad things in the wilderness, the Levites did not join them. God was pleased about this and gave the Levites the honor of serving him as priests. Their job was to lead the people in worshiping their God. There was a lot for the people, as well as the priests, to learn, and *Leviticus* explains what they had to learn.

Numbers includes lists (called a census) of the people who were in the wilderness. The children of Israel had many enemies so the Israelites needed to know how many soldiers they had to fight those enemies. That is why they took the census. God saved the people from their enemies, not because there were so many soldiers or because they were especially good fighters, but because God loved the Israelites and wanted to bring them into a special place called the Promised Land, or Canaan.

Deuteronomy means "second Law." It should not have taken the children of Israel very long to travel from Egypt to the Promised Land. But when they arrived at the border, they were afraid to go in. God had promised to look after them, but they did not believe him. So God said they had to turn back into the wilderness and they stayed there forty years.

Most of the older people who turned back died during these forty years. Young children grew up. So before the Israelites got ready once more to go into the Promised Land, Moses taught them all over again what God had said earlier. *Deuteronomy* repeatedly tells the story about God's loving care and his purposes, or plans, for his people to live together peaceably in Canaan.

LAW

CREATION

Once upon a time there was nothing in the world. Not anything. No trees. No houses. No animals. No bugs. No people. At the very beginning there was no world anywhere. And there were no sun, stars, moons, or planets. No air, no sea. Absolutely nothing.

Everything in the world had a beginning. It came from somewhere and it was made out of something. There was a first tree and a first house and a first spider. Everything had a beginning, except God. He is quite different from anything else. He had no beginning. Nothing made him and he wasn't born. He has always been God and he has always been the same.

God had the idea to make the world. God has such great ideas! He thought of things like giraffes and glowworms. He knew how to make

them and how to make them work. But there was nothing to make them out of. That wasn't a problem to God, though. He knew how to make something out of nothing. Nobody else can do that. What a good thing God was there.

God decided first to make the universe out of nothing. He said in a loud voice, "Let there be light." The most amazing thing happened. The first light happened. Bright, shiny, sparkling light. God saw it and said it was good light. But not all of space was filled with light, because there was also darkness, and God made light and darkness to be separated.

Then God thought of water, so he made some! He did it the same way he made light. He said that there should be something called water and he invented it, and water was all over the place. But everybody

knows you can't let water run all over, so God made some of the water not be water any more. He called what wasn't water anymore, *sky*.

After this God wanted some places that were not wet like water or high like sky. So this is what he did. He pushed a lot of the water back a long way and made dry parts. He called the wet parts *sea* and the dry parts *land*. So now he had light and sea and land and sky. Things were beginning to take shape.

There was a lot of land and God decided to fill it with trees and grass and flowers. He thought of colors like green and blue and red and yellow for all the trees and plants and flowers. It wouldn't have been pretty if every plant and tree had the same color. The flowers would form little seeds that would grow into new plants and flowers. It was a clever plan because not one of the seeds grew up to be anything that it shouldn't have been. Not one little acorn turned into a daisy and no little daisies tried to grow into oak trees.

God looked at the sky and thought it looked far too empty and there was such a lot of it. So he made some bright, shiny lights called stars and planets and some special lights called the sun and the moon. He put them up in the sky and found a way to keep them up there shining brightly.

After God had filled the land with plants, he decided to fill the sea with all sorts of wonderful creatures: big fish and whales, little minnows, lobsters and crabs, ani-mals with shells—zillions of them. Then he made birds that can fly, have pretty feathers, and are great singers. Some birds can both fly and swim, and ostriches can neither fly nor swim but can run very fast. All these interesting creatures had just the right food and right places to live.

God also decided to make all kinds of other wonderful animals to live on the land. Kangaroos jumped, and squirrels ran up trees. Hippopotami lay in quiet river water with just their noses sticking out, and pigs loved rolling in mud. Worms liked wriggling underground, and monkeys had a lot of fun swinging from tree branches.

Then God decided he needed someone who could look after all the things he had made. God had a great idea. He would make a special person who would understand animals and birds and fish and flowers but wouldn't be any of those things. More than that, he would make a person who could get to know God. That would be nice for this special person and nice for God too. Then God would have a friend to love and to talk to. So God made this special person and called him *Adam*. Adam wasn't God and Adam wasn't an animal, and he certainly wasn't a bird or a fish or a flower. He was very special. He was closer to God than anything else God had made and God liked that. Adam liked that too. God and Adam were close friends.

Then Adam noticed something. The monkeys and worms and buttercups and all the other living things were having babies. Adam knew that to have a baby you need a mommy and a daddy, but Adam didn't have someone who could be a mommy. God knew this too because he first thought of babies and mommies and daddies. He thought of everything. So God made a very special person for Adam and he called her *Eve*. Adam was so excited and God was happy for Adam. So now Adam could love Eve as well as God, and Eve could love Adam and God, and God could love them both. There was so much love.

After all this hard work God decided it was time to have a little rest. He wasn't tired. God doesn't get tired. It wasn't nap time. God doesn't nap. He never goes to sleep! He just wanted to take a little break and watch what was going on among all the things he had created. He liked what he had made, and he was very happy. He laughed at the monkeys swinging in the trees and smiled at the baby deer learning to walk on wobbly legs. He listened to whales talking to each other in the depths of the sea. He hummed the tune the wind was making as it blew through the long grass. God saw all that he had made and it was very good.

God saw all that he had made, and it was very good

Genesis 1:31

19

Let's Pretend

Manny and Minny

Manny was a monkey, but he didn't know that. He was the very first monkey. There had never been any monkeys before Manny. God had just made him. Manny had not been born because God had made him. He wasn't a baby and never had been. God made him a full-sized monkey. This was a good idea, because babies need someone to look after them. Since Manny was the first monkey there wasn't a monkey to look after him. God made him so that he could look after himself. Still, it was all very strange and new. Manny had a lot of things to learn about being a monkey.

From where he was sitting Manny could see something bright and shiny. It was water, but Manny didn't know that. He decided to have a look at it. He got up and started to walk, but it was difficult. He had two very long legs and two very long arms but the arms were not as long as the legs. He tried walking on his two long legs. That worked fine. Then he tried walking using his arms like legs. That worked very well too. So he walked both ways.

Manny came to the water and saw bright little fish darting around. *That looks like fun,* he thought. He jumped in the water with a great splash. This scared him, and he began to sink. But he managed to scramble out and lay on the bank gasping for breath.

I can't do what those bright things do, he said to himself. *I wish I was like them.* He sat by the water and watched the fish. Then he saw something else. It was his reflection, but he didn't know that was what it was. He thought it was something behind him. He jumped up and looked around. Nothing was there! He looked in the water again. There it was again! He looked to one side. The thing in the water did the same. He looked the other way. It looked the other way. *The thing is doing what I do,* he thought. It took Manny a long time to learn that he was looking at himself and that he had two great big eyes and a mouth full of big white teeth.

At that moment a blue and green bird began to sing. It sat high in a tree. Manny heard the singing and saw the bird, but he didn't know it was a bird because he'd never seen one before. He wanted a closer look so he began to climb the tree. Higher and higher he climbed. With his strong hands he held on to the branches.

Once he slipped, but he grabbed a branch with his tail and hung upside down. This was scary at first; then he thought it was fun. He began to swing by his tail faster and faster until he was swinging so far he came near to the next tree. He was so excited about this that he forgot to hold on tightly with his tail. He flew off the branch, high in the air, and grabbed another branch on the next tree as he went past.

Manny's heart was beating very quickly, and he sat on the branch to think about what had happened. *I can't do what the bright things do in the splashy place* (he meant fish and water of course, but he didn't know what to call them), *but I can climb and swing and walk two different ways, and I have two big brown eyes and big white teeth,* he thought. Manny was finding out what it meant to be a monkey.

Suddenly Manny noticed something strange. On the next tree an animal was swinging. It had brown eyes and white teeth. It was swinging high. *That must be me,* Manny thought. It wasn't, of course. It was Minny, another monkey God had made. Manny started to swing on his branch. Closer and closer he came to where Minny was swinging. Then with a great leap, he let go and flew in the air and landed beside her. That's how

Manny and Minny met each other. They looked alike and did things the same way, and they liked each other.

Later some little monkeys were born to Manny and Minny. They showed the baby monkeys how to walk and swing in the trees and how not to fall in the water. God had given the baby monkeys parents who loved them and helped them to grow up.

GOD'S WORLD & ME

God had made a marvelous world for people to live in. He wanted us to enjoy it, so he made sure we had eyes to see the tops of the highest mountains, waves on the oceans, and smiles on the faces of people who love us. He gave us ears so we could hear the songs of the birds, the honking of geese, and the barking of dogs. Our ears can even hear what our eyes cannot see, like the wind rustling the leaves of the trees. God gave us noses to smell roses, hot popcorn, and pizza. He gave us tongues to taste popsicles, candy, and hamburgers! God made so many interesting things for us to touch as well—the softness of a kitten's ear, poky pine needles, bread dough, and water, sand, and pebbles. Best of all, God made us able to say *thank you* for all these wonderful things.

When Adam was created in the beginning of things, he knew nothing about gummy bears, soccer, skateboards, TV cartoons, string cheese, bicycles, or kites. But he did know a lot about animals.

God had formed the animals and placed them in the Garden of Eden, and he gave Adam the job of naming all the animals. If God asked you to name a giraffe, a lion, or a rhinoceros, what would you name them?

Adam didn't have lights in his house, or even candles, but God had hung millions of night lights in the sky to twinkle so it wouldn't be dark.

The Bible does not tell us if Adam gave names to the sun, moon, and stars. Maybe he did. But no one could give names to all the stars. God created so many billions of stars, and some are so far away that astronomers today with the most powerful telescopes have not seen nearly all of them. They can't possibly know how many there are and how far space, or the universe, reaches. But God knows. God is bigger than the universe he made and so great that he can count and name all the stars (Psalm 147:4).

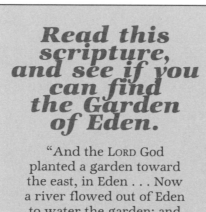

THIS IS GARY GNAT.
WE INTERRUPT THIS BOOK
WITH A SPECIAL REPORT FROM
OUR
BUZZY-BODY REPORTER,
BARBRA ZITT.
TAKE IT AWAY, BARBRA!

Where was the Garden of Eden?

The Bible gives us some hints about where the Garden of Eden was, even though we don't know for sure. Adam could have bathed in the Tigris River or sometimes in the Euphrates River. And he could have climbed mountains such as the Zagros Mountains, Mount Sinai, Mount Zion, Mount Ararat, and Mount Carmel. See if you can find these on a map or globe.

Read this scripture, and see if you can find the Garden of Eden.

"And the LORD God planted a garden toward the east, in Eden . . . Now a river flowed out of Eden to water the garden; and from there it divided and became four rivers . . . The name of the first is Pishon; it flows around the whole land of Havilah, . . . where there is gold. . . . And the name of the second river is Gihon; it flows around the whole land of Cush. And the name of the third river is Tigris; it flows east of Assyria. And the fourth river is the Euphrates."

Genesis 2:8–14 (NASB)

Mediterranean Sea

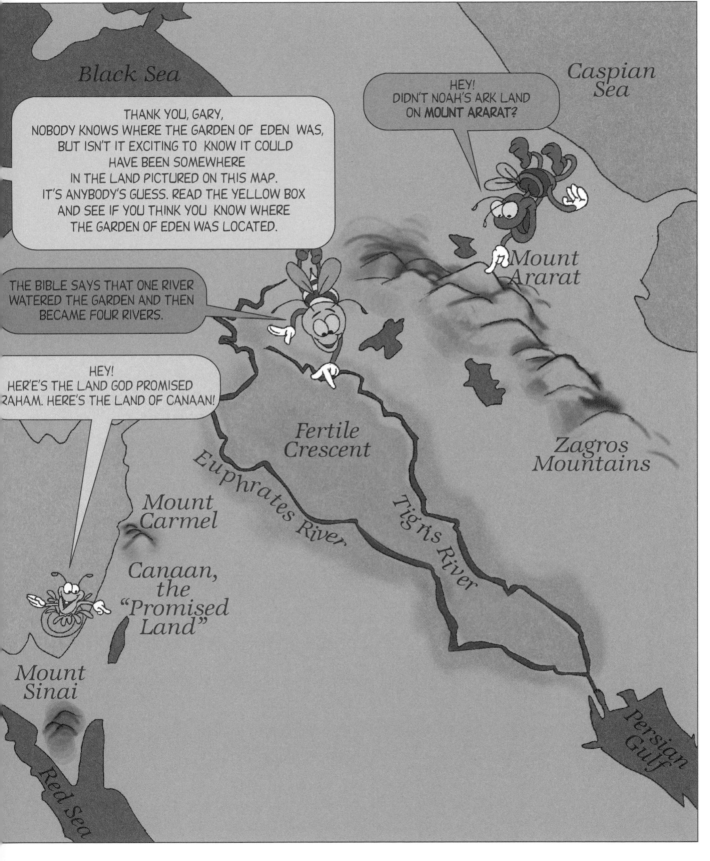

PARTICIPANTS ARE ENCOURAGED TO EXPAND AND IMPROVISE, USING THIS MATERIAL AS A GUIDE. ALLOW YOUR IMAGINATION TO "PEEK AROUND THE CORNER OF THE VERSE" AND SEE WHO IS COMING.

OPEN YOUR MOUTH REEEALLY WIDE AND SAY, "PEEEEEK"!

Your Family Video Theater

Very, Very Good

Cast: Little Cloud, Cloud Chorus (3 speakers, in unison), Tree, Flower, Giraffe, Ant, Mountain, Wondermaker (voice only). The characters could wear masks.

Little Cloud   Hello, everyone, I'm Little Cloud.

Cloud Chorus   Hello, Little Cloud, you look so pretty today.

Tree   The sun is making all your edges pink.

Flower   What can you see, Little Cloud?

Little Cloud   Everything! Big mountains and deep, deep valleys. Wide oceans and rolling hills. The Wondermaker has made it all perfectly bright and beautiful.

Cloud Chorus   Praise the Wondermaker!

Tree   And what will you do today, Little Cloud?

Little Cloud   I don't know yet. Today I may just stay still and watch you play, or I may join my brothers and sisters to bring cooling shadows over the hot ground, or I may climb on the shoulders of my mother and father till I am high in the sky and you can hardly see me.

Flower   It must be so much fun being a little cloud.

Little Cloud   And what will you do today, Flower?

Flower   I'll dance when the wind comes by and smile at the sun in the sky and I'll be pretty and smell sweet so the busy bees will carry my seeds away and make more of me.

Little Cloud	That sounds like fun. Just look at that giraffe. What a looooooong neck. Hello! Hello!
Giraffe	Hello, Little Cloud, can you see my spots?
Little Cloud	If I come down near the earth I can. What will you do today?
Giraffe	I'll count my spots and then I'll count my wife's spots too. All my family may count their spots because we've just discovered there's not one of us the same. Can you imagine, all our spots are different.
Cloud Chorus	Such variety—praise the Wondermaker!
Ant	Hello, Little Cloud. Can you see me now that you are so close to the earth?
Little Cloud	Sure, I can see you, Ant. What will you do today?
Ant	I'm much too busy to stop what I'm doing to tell you.
Little Cloud	*(laughing)* Oh, my, look at you all. Thousands of you scuttering around making your ant hill higher and higher.
Cloud Chorus	How clever you are, Wondermaker, that you have made such tiny creatures to do such grand things.
Little Cloud	Hello, Mountain! How tall you are. May I sit on your head for a while or wrap myself around your neck like a scarf?
Mountain	Hello, Little Cloud. Sit on my head if you like. I have a headache from the hot sun and you can cool me down.
Little Cloud	What will you do today, Mountain?
Mountain	I'll just be me. I'm big and strong, I'll remind all of you little things of our great God who is big and strong too.
All characters	How strong is the Wondermaker. How great! How mighty!
Wondermaker's voice	Hello, Creation. Are you busy being clouds, mountains, hills, valleys, trees, giraffes, tiny ants, and pretty flowers?
All characters	Yes, yes, Wondermaker. Thank you for creating us. We love being us. We want to praise you.
Wondermaker's voice	I am happy. I have made all things very, very good.

Thank You, God

Words and Music by
Stuart Briscoe and Larry Moore

Moderately

1. Thank You, God, for bright blue sky, for fluf-fy clouds where birds can fly. Thank You,
2. Thank You, God, for sway-ing trees, for rust-ling leaves in gen-tle breeze. Thank You,
3. Thank You, God, for trees and nest, for branch to perch and place to rest. Thank You,

God, for pret-ty fea-thers that keep them warm in chil-ly wea-ther. Thank You,
God, for pleas-ant show-ers that fill the earth with love-ly flow-ers.
God, for young that tweet, for jui-cy worms for them to eat.

God, for songs to sing. Thank You, God, for

3rd time to Coda

ev - ery - thing.

rit.

ADAM AND EVE

God loved Adam and his wife, Eve, very much. God wanted them to love him too. He was their heavenly Father, and they were his children. Good, loving children do what their parents ask them to do. So God asked Adam and Eve to be good, to be obedient.

People can be obedient in two ways. First, they do what they are told to do. Second, they keep from doing what they are told not to do. God had told Adam and Eve to do lots of things, but only one thing not to do. God said they must not eat fruit from one particular tree. To disobey would be very bad, and they would have to leave the beautiful garden where they lived. God wanted his children to live happily with him in the garden. If they did not obey him, they could not be happy, and neither could God.

The angels, whom God had also made, were to be obedient too. They lived with God in heaven. They had lots of things to do and some things not to do. One certain angel, Lucifer, was not obedient. He wanted to be greater than God. So God sent him out of heaven, and he became God's enemy.

One day Lucifer, whose name had been changed to Satan, met Eve at the special tree. Satan said it would be all right if she had some of the fruit. Eve didn't think so, but Satan said it would be a good idea. He told her the fruit would make her very wise and God would like that. Eve thought that sounded good. Besides, the fruit was beautiful food, so she ate some. She also gave some to Adam. He knew that he should not eat it, but he did anyway. Immediately Adam and Eve knew

33

tried to hide from God, but that was impossible. They had both done something that showed they did not love God with their whole hearts. This is called the fall.

So God sent them out of the garden. Life became very difficult for them. They wandered far away from God.

But God still loved Adam and Eve. So God made a plan. He thought of a way to punish someone else and forgive them. He told Adam and Eve that his plan was for them to have children, who would have children, and so on. And one day God himself would become one of those children. He would be strong enough to fight Satan and win the world back to himself. This God-child would be named Jesus. When he grew up, he would be punished instead of Adam and Eve and their ch

Adam and Eve were happy about God's plan. Sin was making a terrible mess of God's world and they were sorry for what they had done. They told their children about the promised God-child, who told their children, who told their children.

And we know that's exactly what happened. Now God will forgive us and allow us to come into heaven when we die. How God made this happen is the story of the whole Bible.

Let's Pretend

THIS IS A STORY TOLD AS FANTASY MARRIED TO FACT TO BE MIXED WITH FAITH AND LAUGHTER, LOVE AND JOY.

LOUDER! WIGGLE THOSE TONSILS. RATTLE THOSE GUMS.

Everything in the garden was lovely. The sun shone brightly. The breeze gently swayed the trees. A bright red bird high on a branch sang for joy, and two white doves joined in the song. The flowers nodded their colored heads, and their sweet perfume filled the air. On the pond ripples chased each other to the grassy banks. Shiny fish jumped high and disappeared with a splash and a plop. A lion that hadn't learned how to be fierce and a lamb that didn't know how to be frightened played catch with a juicy orange pumpkin.

Adam and Eve were happy. They had just eaten a lunch of fresh fruit and nuts and drunk water from a small gurgling stream. Eve liked apples and pears, but

Adam liked oranges and luscious pomegranates. Of course, these fruits didn't have little name tags on them. Adam had given them names. God had made many different kinds of food. Adam and Eve had to be careful not to eat too much, because there was work to be done. Except today. Today was rest day. God had rested after making everything; he told Adam to work six days and rest one day. That gave Adam time to think and to thank God for his goodness. Of course, Adam and Eve were thankful every day, but the seventh day was special.

Adam thought he would go for a walk while Eve slept peacefully. He made his way past the lion and the lamb and smiled to himself. Adam noticed brightly colored dragonflies hovering over the pond. Every day he saw something new. He started to climb a small hill. It was one of his favorite places. From the top he could see a long way.

On top of the hill was a tree. This tree was different. It had a white fence round it. Adam had never seen any other fence and didn't know what it was for. You don't need fences in a garden like Eden where nobody is going to harm anyone or steal anything.

35

One evening Adam had asked God about the fence. He wasn't sure if he liked it. But God had explained why it was there. God always has a reason for what he does.

"Adam," God said, "I love you very much."

"I know that, Master," Adam replied, "and I love you too."

"How do you know that I love you, Adam?" God asked.

"Well, Master, you keep telling me that you love me, and you have given me so many wonderful things to enjoy."

"So you know I love you by the things I say . . ."

"Yes," Adam interrupted (which he shouldn't really have done) "and by the things that you do."

"That's right, Adam. We show our love by the things that we do and by the things that we don't do."

"I understand all this, Master," Adam replied, "but I don't understand the fence around the tree."

"I'm coming to that," God said. "I put that tree there with a fence around it because you are not to touch it."

"But why not, God?" Adam asked, hoping that God wouldn't mind him asking such questions. "It is such a beautiful tree and the fruit looks delicious."

"Because you have to show you love me," God replied. "And I gave you a way that's not very hard. Just don't eat anything from that tree. That will show that you love me."

"That's fine," Adam replied. "Thank you for giving me such a simple way to show that I love you."

Adam often came to the tree with the fence around it. Every time Adam looked at the tree and walked away from it he said in his heart, "Are you watching, Master? I hope so. I'm walking past the tree to show I love you."

Now Adam walked on again as he had before, happy that he loved God. But suddenly a very strange thing happened. There was a bright flash in the sky, then a loud noise. Adam didn't know about lightning and thunder. Some dark clouds moved in front of the sun. Adam shivered. He wasn't dressed for chill winds. It was most unpleasant. Adam was unsure of what was happening and thought, *I must ask God about this the next time we talk*.

Eve felt the chill wind too. It awakened her. Standing near her was a creature she had never seen before. He smiled pleasantly at her. "Good afternoon," he said. This was very strange because he looked like a beautiful, brilliantly colored serpent. Eve thought she had never seen anything so beautiful and handsome. But the creature was speaking in a language she understood. Serpents didn't usually do that. Only God and Adam did that.

"Would you like to go for a walk?" he asked.

"Certainly." She smiled, leaping to her feet. They set off past the pond and started to climb the hill. The creature walked quite fast, seeming to glide over the ground without effort. Eve struggled to keep up with him. When they arrived at the top of the hill, Eve sat down on the grass to catch her breath. The creature walked toward the white fence.

"I don't know your name," Eve shouted to him.

"Oh, you can call me Satan or Devil or Serpent. Whatever you wish," he replied.

"I never saw you before," Eve said. "Why do you have so many names?"

"Well, I used to be called Lucifer but I recently had a job change. I used to work in heaven with God, but we had a disagreement, and I was fired. He threw me out. I think he was unfair. Did you see the lightning and hear the thunder? That was me being thrown out of heaven."

"What are you going to do now that you are out of work?" Eve asked.

"I'm going to straighten out things on earth. I don't think God is handling the world properly," he replied. Eve had never heard such talk. It made her uncomfortable. But she was a little excited as well. She wondered what Adam would have said. *What is this creature?* she thought.

"Take this fence, for instance." Satan said. "Why put such an ugly thing around such a beautiful tree?"

"Oh, I know the answer to that," Eve said quickly. "It's there so that we can show we love God by doing what he says. He told us not to touch the tree. We love God, so we do what he said. We don't mind the fence."

"I think the fence is ugly. Anyway, what did God say would happen if you ate some of the fruit?"

"He said we would die," Eve answered, although she didn't know what "die" meant. Adam had said it was very unpleasant, so she knew dying was not nice.

"You won't die," shouted the serpent. "You'll grow up. You'll be better people. God is keeping something from you like he kept things from me. He wouldn't let me do what I wanted, and he's doing the same to you." With that he leaped over the fence with the greatest of ease, reached up, took a beautiful piece of fruit, and with another graceful leap landed beside Eve. "Here, take a bite. It won't do you any harm. It will do you good," he said with a mischievous grin.

Eve was confused. The fruit looked so good, she didn't know what "die" meant, the serpent was so wise and beautiful, and she loved the way he leaped over fences. She liked the idea of eating fruit that would be good for her. She wished Adam would come back and then she thought, *I'm perfectly able to think for myself without him.* She held the fruit and took a great bite. The serpent jumped high in the air for joy. Then he turned quickly and without a word glided down the hill, laughing as he went, until he disappeared among the trees.

It was the sweetest fruit that Eve had ever tasted, but it left a bitter taste. It was very juicy, but her mouth was dry. The trees started to spin around, and the sun flashed in her eyes. She had never felt dizzy. Her knees were weak, so she sat down quickly. Just then Adam came striding up the hill. When he saw Eve he could feel something was wrong.

"Are you all right?" he asked Eve.

"Never felt better," she lied, never having done that before.

"You look different," Adam replied.

"I am different. I'm smarter, I'm freer, I'm a more interesting person!" she said quickly and rose to her feet. Then to Adam's amazement she jumped over the fence, trying to imitate the serpent.

"Come back!" Adam shouted at the top of his voice. "You should not be in there."

"Come and get me," she laughed.

Before Adam could do anything, she took a piece of fruit, climbed back over the fence, and with a grin said, "While you were gone I met the most interesting creature who said his name was, among other things, Satan. He used to work for God, but God wasn't being fair, so Satan came down to earth to put things right. He told me that we had every right to eat this fruit and it would do us good and we would be better people. So I had some, and he was right. You must take a bite, Adam. It tastes sweet and it's so smooth and delicious."

Adam looked at his beautiful wife. He loved her so much, and she wanted him to join her in eating the fruit. He had to show that he loved her. All she was asking him to do was take one bite of a delicious piece of fruit. But God had said no. He loved God very much and he loved Eve very much. Did he love the things God had given him more than he loved God? He knew that couldn't be right. But he could see Eve and hold her, and he couldn't see God or hold him. So, knowing very well that he should not do it, he bit into the fruit.

It was as if the world stood still. Birds stopped singing, animals stopped playing, fish stopped jumping, and the wind stopped blowing. Then Adam and Eve knew that God was there with them. They could not see him, but they knew. They rushed behind some trees and tried to hide. But he knew where they were. You can't hide from God.

"It wasn't my fault," Adam said. "Eve made me do it. And you gave her to me."

"It wasn't my fault," Eve said hurriedly. "The serpent made me do it."

"Serpent, come back here," said God in a loud voice. The serpent appeared from behind the trees. He wasn't gliding anymore.

"What you have done is very wrong," God said sternly. "You must be punished. You will cause trouble and you will be troubled, and one day you will be defeated. You, Eve, will have great pain in your life, and Adam, you will find this world a hard place to live in. What you have done is much more than bite a piece of fruit. You have disobeyed me, and when you do that, everything goes wrong. Now you cannot live in the garden. You must leave immediately."

So Adam and his wife walked slowly away. Thorns tore at their legs. It was cold, and they shivered. A storm ripped at the tops of the trees. Birds hurried for shelter, little animals hid behind trees as they went past, and big animals growled at them. The lion and lamb were not playing anymore because the lamb was dead, torn in pieces by the lion—her former friend. "What have we done?" said Adam and Eve as they left the garden. A mosquito stung Adam on his neck. Life was starting to be hard.

"WHERE ARE YOU?" THE LORD GOD CALLED TO THE MAN

Genesis 3:19

ADAM, EVE, & ME

How sad that Adam and Eve passed along their sinful nature to us. God needs to make our hearts clean again because all of us make sinful choices just like Adam and Eve. God loved Adam and Eve and all their children (and that includes us) so much that he sent the Lord Jesus to be the way our sins could be forgiven. One day Jesus will take us home to heaven, which is an even more lovely place to live than the Garden of Eden. Wouldn't you like to go there? Thank Jesus for coming to our planet to pay for our sins. Jesus had to die on the cross to make all this possible, but now he is safe in heaven waiting for us to join him there. And because he is God, he hears our prayers. Do you know what to say to him? Maybe it would help you to use the prayer below.

Dear Jesus,

I think it's really sad Adam and Eve sinned, because it spoiled everything for all of us. Now we all know how to sin—and do it. But thank you for making a way that I can be forgiven and come to live with you when I die. Please send your Spirit into my heart right now so that I can be your loving child. And thank you for dying for me on the cross to make it all possible.

Amen.

If you prayed this prayer you might want to write the prayer on a separate piece of paper and sign your name and write the date to remind you of this important time in your life.

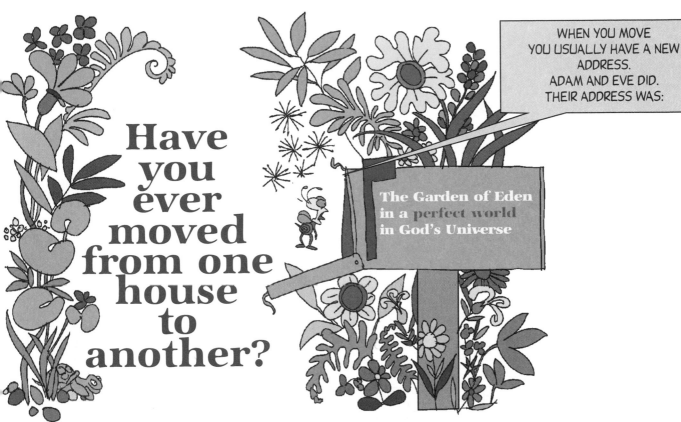

WHEN YOU MOVE YOU USUALLY HAVE A NEW ADDRESS. ADAM AND EVE DID. THEIR ADDRESS WAS:

The Garden of Eden in a perfect world in God's Universe

Have you ever moved from one house to another?

NOW THEIR ADDRESS IS:

East of Eden Land of Nod in a spoiled world in God's Universe

Have you ever moved from one house to another? Remember all the packing and sorting out and putting things in boxes you had to do? What fun to go to a new place, meet new friends, explore new playplaces, and start all over again. But it was different when the first moving day happened. Adam and Eve, the very first people who moved, were very, very unhappy. They were being moved out of their lovely garden to a wild place that wasn't half as nice as their garden. There were weeds and thistles and all sorts of dangers they had never thought about before. They didn't want to leave the garden but God said they had to leave. That's what happens when we sin. Things usually aren't half as nice as they used to be.

41

A BIG PILE OF
BIRTHDAY
CAKES

The families of Adam and Eve's children and great-great-grandchildren lived a long, long, long time.

But even though they lived very, very, very long, they died one day,

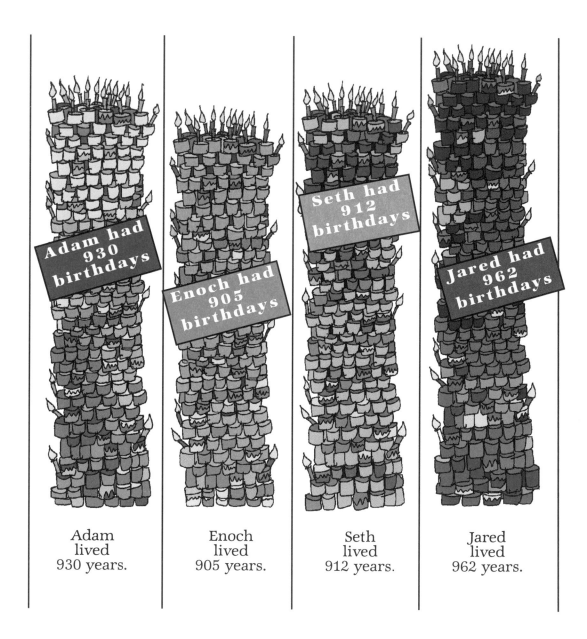

Adam had 930 birthdays

Enoch had 905 birthdays

Seth had 912 birthdays

Jared had 962 birthdays

Adam
lived
930 years.

Enoch
lived
905 years.

Seth
lived
912 years.

Jared
lived
962 years.

just as God said they would, because sin had come into the world.

Think of the oldest person you know. How old is he or she—50, 60, 70, 80? Just imagine people more than ten times older than someone you know who is 80 years old.

Would they have lots of wrinkes? Would their hair be white?

If they had birthday cakes in those days like we do today, imagine how long it would have taken someone to light all the candles—and blow them out!

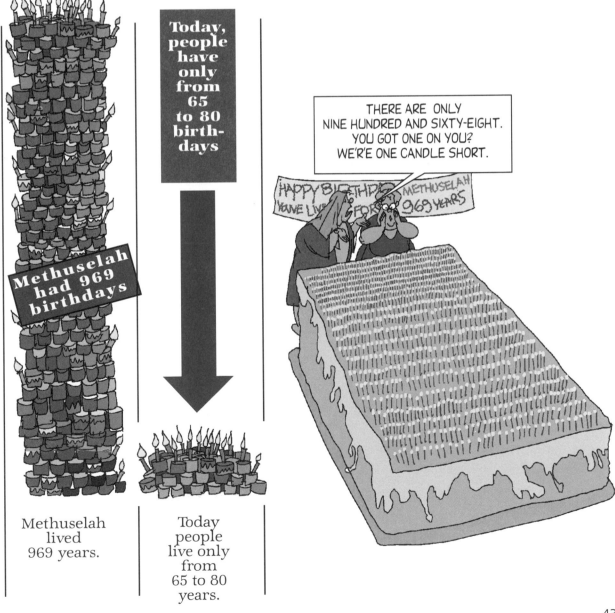

Today, people have only from 65 to 80 birth-days

Methuselah had 969 birthdays

Methuselah lived 969 years.

Today people live only from 65 to 80 years.

THERE ARE ONLY NINE HUNDRED AND SIXTY-EIGHT. YOU GOT ONE ON YOU? WE'R'E ONE CANDLE SHORT.

PARTICIPANTS ARE ENCOURAGED TO EXPAND AND IMPROVISE, USING THIS MATERIAL AS A GUIDE. ALLOW YOUR IMAGINATION TO "PEEK AROUND THE CORNER OF THE VERSE" AND SEE WHO IS COMING.

Let's Make a Video about

SAY IT AGAIN, AND

AGAIN AND

AGAIN,

The Birds

Your Family Video Theater

Cast: Redbird and two white doves—Snowwhite and Offwhite

Scene: A treetop five minutes after the fall

Redbird   I don't feel like singing anymore.

Offwhite   Me neither.

Snowwhite   Me neither.

Offwhite   I just said that.

Snowwhite   I just said it too.

Offwhite   Do you always have to repeat what I say?

Snowwhite   No. In fact, I've never done it before.

Offwhite   Well, don't do it again.

Snowwhite   I will if I want to.

Offwhite   Then find another branch to sit on.

(Snowwhite flies across to the branch where Redbird is sitting.)

Redbird   What do you want?

Snowwhite   I just want to sit quietly on this branch.

Redbird   It's my branch! I don't want to share it.

Snowwhite   But I want to stay close to some bird. Offwhite
               doesn't want me.

Redbird   I don't want you either.

Snowwhite   Why is every bird getting their feathers ruf-
               fled? We used to love each other and now
               we're being mean to each other.

Offwhite   You started it by repeating everything I said.

Redbird   That's right. And you came to my branch without being invited.

Snowwhite	I'm sorry. I didn't mean to be difficult. Can't we just be friends like we used to be? Let's sing that song we used to sing." (Sings *Thank You, God* from Creation story.)

> Thank You, God, for bright blue sky,
> For fluffy clouds where birds can fly.
> Thank You, God, for pretty feathers
> That keep them warm in chilly weather.
> Thank You, God, for songs to sing.
> Thank You, God, for everything.

Redbird	Stop that. I told you I didn't feel like singing.
Snowwhite	But you've always been such a great singer.
Redbird	I'm not anymore. Anyway, I sing only when I'm happy, and I'm not happy.
Snowwhite	But didn't God make us to sing whether we're happy or not? Didn't God make us so that we could fill the earth with music?
Redbird	I don't like being told what to do by God or by anybird else. If I feel like singing I'll sing, and if I don't I won't.
Offwhite	That goes for me too. I feel as if I've grown up. I feel free to be me.
Snowwhite	Where did you learn to think like that?
Redbird	While you were gone we heard Adam and Eve talking.
Offwhite	And they decided that they were not going to do just what God wanted them to do. And to show that they meant it, they ate the fruit from the tree.
Redbird	That's right. God wasn't happy and sent them away. But I think they are free now.
Offwhite	And that's what we're going to be.
Snowwhite	But isn't this bad for all of us?
Redbird	How can it be bad for us?
Snowwhite	You just said you weren't happy. And you didn't feel like singing. And we started being mean to each other. And you don't want to please God anymore.
Offwhite	It may be bad for you. But we think it's good for us. Come on, Redbird, let's get out of here. Let's see if we can find Adam and Eve. (*Redbird and Offwhite fly away.*)
Snowwhite	(*watching them go says sadly*) They want to find Adam and Eve and be free like them. I want to find God and be happy again. I want to sing again.

NOAH

Long ago, and many years after God had made the world, the people of the world made God very sad. All of them, except for one family, were doing what Satan wanted them to do. They never thought about God, and they were cruel to each other, doing whatever they felt like doing.

God looked over the world and said, "Why did I ever make all these people?" But as he looked this way and that at all the evil things going on, he saw a very special man named Noah. Noah was not doing evil things. He was doing good things.

"Why, there's a man and his family who are trying to be good," God said. "I'll save them and destroy all the others. Then I'll start all over again with Noah's family. And after lots of years, the God-child Jesus will be born of his family."

So God decided he would send an awful lot of rain, until the rivers and lakes and oceans overflowed. Then the whole world would be flooded with water. All life would end except for Noah and his family. God also decided to save a Mr. and Mrs. (a male and a female) of every animal, bird, and bug on the earth.

Before he destroyed all the bad people, God warned them. He loved all the people so much his heart hurt. Noah would tell the people about God who loved them and about how much his family loved God. Noah would preach to the people.

The Bible says God was very patient and waited for at least a hundred years for people to say they were sorry. But no one listened to Noah.

God helped Mr. Noah and his sons, whose names were Shem, Ham, and Japheth, to build a big, big, BIG boat called an ark. It took Noah a long time to build the ark according to the plans God gave him.

Noah never gave up. If anyone asked him about the boat he was building, he explained about the flood that God was going to send. If

anyone told Noah he was silly to build it or made fun of him, he paid no attention.

At last the ark was ready, and God helped Mr. Noah's family find two of every living thing on the whole earth and bring them inside. God had told Noah to store food in the ark. Finally all were safely inside.

The rain began to fall. It came, and came, and came, and came! All life on earth died—except the eight people and the animals and bugs in the ark. The water reached over the top of the highest mountain.

After ten days, and another ten, and another ten, and another ten, the rain stopped. Then it took one whole year and ten more days before the land was dry enough for everyone to come out of the ark.

Noah's family and all the animals, birds, and bugs were very, very, very, VERY happy to get out of the ark and begin to live on the "new" earth.

That day Mr. Noah's family thanked God for saving them and promised him they would be good. Then God promised he never again would send such a terrible flood to destroy the whole world. He said all the seasons— spring, summer, autumn, and winter—would come in the right order every year.

While the family thought about that, a beautiful rainbow reached from the clouds to the ground. God said that every time a rainbow comes he will remember all his promises to Noah and to the world.

God always keeps his promises to all of us.

NOAH & ME

It's hard to be laughed at, isn't it? People probably laughed at Noah, and that would have hurt his feelings.

Think about this. The boat God asked him to build was as long as one and one-half football fields and as high as four houses stacked together. And there wasn't even a very large lake anywhere nearby. The people who watched Noah

build this huge boat on dry land must have thought he was weird!

It's hard when your friends think you're odd just because you're a Christian and don't always do the things they do. When that happens, it's good to talk to God about it. Noah told God about his feelings and his worries, and that helped. It will help you too.

Let's Pretend

THIS IS A STORY TOLD AS FANTASY MARRIED TO FACT

YOU'VE GOT IT.

TO BE MIXED WITH FAITH AND LAUGHTER, LOVE AND, AND, AND. . .

THAT'S IT, YES, YES. YEEEEEEES,

AND. . . JJJOY.

AAAGH! YOU BLEW IT! YOU BLEW IT"

ANIMAL FUR MAKES MRS. NOAH SNEEZE

"What's the matter, Dear?" Mrs. Noah asked her husband. "You look worried."

Mr. Noah *was* worried. He knew his wife didn't like animals. But God had told him to build a boat called an ark and take two of every kind of animal on board.

"What's the matter, Dear?" Mrs. Noah asked again.

"Would you like a cat for your birthday?" Mr. Noah asked hopefully.

"A cat!" Mrs. Noah replied in amazement. "You know I'm allergic to cats. And *other* animals!"

Oh, dear, thought Mr. Noah. *How would she ever manage to live in a zoo?*

The next day their son Shem came by to help build the boat God had told Mr. Noah to build. When Shem got off his camel he had a tummyache. That made his father worry.

"What's the matter, Father?" Shem asked. "You look worried."

Mr. Noah *was* worried. He knew Shem was sick because riding a camel always made his tummy ache.

Oh, dear, thought Mr. Noah. *What will happen when the boat is rocking on the sea? Shem is bound to get motion sickness.*

Their second son, Ham, came by to bring some sandwiches and fresh corn and cheese from his farm for lunch. Mr. Noah invited Ham into the kitchen, but he wouldn't come inside.

"What's the matter, Father?" Ham asked. "You look worried."

Mr. Noah *was* worried. He knew Ham lived outside in a big tent and that he couldn't stand being cooped up in a small space like

49

the kitchen. It gave Ham a "shut-in" feeling. We call that feeling by a long word—*claustrophobia.*

Oh, dear, thought Mr. Noah. *How will Ham ever manage being shut up in the ark for a long time?*

Mr. Noah's third son, Japheth, came round the corner and greeted him. Japheth's wife was with him, and she had just found out she was going to have a baby.

"What's the matter, Father," Japheth asked. "You look worried." "I *am* worried," replied Mr. Noah. He looked at Japheth's wife and wondered how they would manage without a doctor on board. What would happen if the baby was born while they were alone in the ark with nothing but water everywhere?

Mr. Noah talked to God about all his concerns.

"What's the matter?" asked God. "You look worried."

So Mr. Noah told God how worried he was about Mrs. Noah, who didn't like animals and was allergic to cats. He talked to him about Shem, who got motion sickness easily. He told God about Ham, who didn't like being shut up in small places. He talked to him about Japheth's wife, who was going to have a baby.

And then Noah told God about his biggest worry of all. "You know I failed woodworking at school," he said. "I always hit my thumb with the hammer. And I don't know how to make the door of the ark watertight so we won't all drown. I'll never be able to build a boat like you want me to!" he ended, feeling really miserable.

God told Mr. Noah to stop worrying and cheer up. God said he would help everyone be strong and brave. He would also help them with their sneezes, tummy-aches, closed-in feelings, and even having a baby in an ark afloat on a huge flood.

"What's more," God said, "I've made some detailed plans to help you know how to build the big boat. And I myself will seal the door shut from outside, once you are all safely inside."

"But if you shut the door from the outside, we'll be all alone inside," objected Mr. Noah, more worried than ever.

God smiled and told Mr. Noah to stop worrying right away.

"I'm God! I can be outside and inside all at the same time!" he assured Noah.

Mr. Noah stopped worrying and got very excited about the whole project. He went back to his family and told them everything God had told him. Mrs. Noah, Shem, Ham, and Japheth and their wives also stopped worrying and thanked God for saving them from the wickedness on earth.

They sat down together and ate the sandwiches Ham had brought for lunch. They tasted very good, indeed!

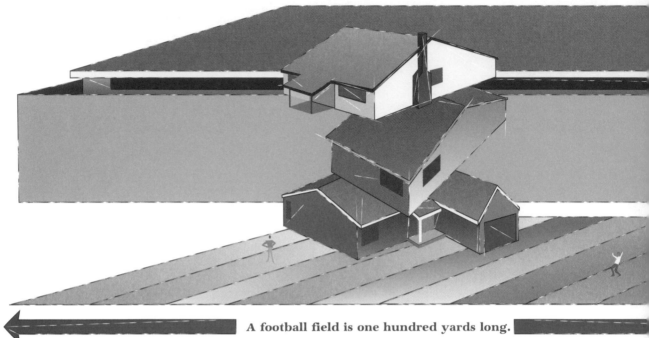

A football field is one hundred yards long.

The meaning of the word *ark* is "a chest" or "vessel to float." NOAH'S ARK is the boat God told Noah to build so he could escape the coming flood (Genesis 6:14–16).

Noah was told to use gopher wood to build the ark which would be 450 feet long, 75 feet wide, and 45 feet high. That's six times longer than it is wide. There was to be an open window all around the top part of the ark, 18 inches below the roof. Noah was to put a large door in

the side of the ark. It took Noah and his three sons, Shem, Ham, and Japheth, many, many, many years to build the ark.

Have you ever been on a boat? What sort of a boat? It probably wasn't a boat like the one Noah built. There has been only one of those. Did the boat you sailed on have a rudder? A rudder helps you to turn right or left. Noah's boat didn't have a rudder. It didn't have a sail either. That's because it wasn't

WHAT IS PITCH?

PITCH IS A STICKY-GOOEY STUFF NOAH SLOPPED BETWEEN THE BOARDS TO KEEP WATER OUT.

Fancy Footnotes

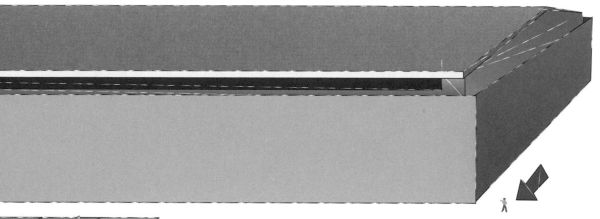

This is you
standing next to
Noah's ark.

The ark was one and one half
football fields long.

going anywhere! Most boats go
somewhere but Noah's just
FLOATED on the waves.

Most boats have a reason for
being boats.

What does a tug boat do?
a submarine
a battleship
a speedboat

Noah's boat had a reason too. It
was built to protect Noah and his
family and all the animals and
insects God saved from the flood.

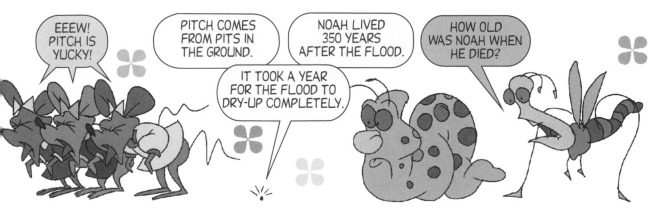

EEEW!
PITCH IS
YUCKY!

PITCH COMES
FROM PITS IN
THE GROUND.

NOAH LIVED
350 YEARS
AFTER THE FLOOD.

HOW OLD
WAS NOAH WHEN
HE DIED?

IT TOOK A YEAR
FOR THE FLOOD TO
DRY-UP COMPLETELY.

53

If a boat springs a leak today, sailors try to fix it with plastic. Noah didn't use plastic because it hadn't been invented. He painted the ark with pitch. Pitch is like tar. It was dug from pits in the ground where it was soft, but it got hard in the air.

Why do you think there were no fish tanks on board? That's right. The fish didn't drown in the flood— they loved it! Just imagine what fun it was to go fishing right out your window!

These were some of the fruits in Mrs. Noah's pantry: grapes, melons, figs, dates, pomegranates. Which do you recognize?

These were some of the veggies: beans, lentils, onions, cucumbers, gourds. Which would you have chosen for dinner?

When they wanted a drink, they could milk a cow. It must have been hard to do when the wind was blowing and the waters were rough.

54

When your mom or dad thinks about making a meal for your family, how many people do they cook for? 2? 4? 6? 8? Imagine making food for eight people and all the animals in the ark! Even with eight people helping, it must have been a lot of work.

AND THEY DID IT FOR 415 DAYS!

When the time came for the flood to dry up, Noah's boat didn't have a pier to be tied to; it was on a mountain. The Bible says the ark came to rest on the "mountains of Ararat" (Genesis 8:4). The present-day country of Turkey has a range of mountains known as Ararat. These mountains might be the place mentioned in the Bible, but we're not sure. Even to this day no one has ever found the ark of Noah. Do you think that's one of God's secrets?

Noah was old, really old, when he died at age 950. He lived 350 years after the flood.

GOD COMMANDED NOAH DID EVERYTHING JUST AS HIM

Genesis 6:22

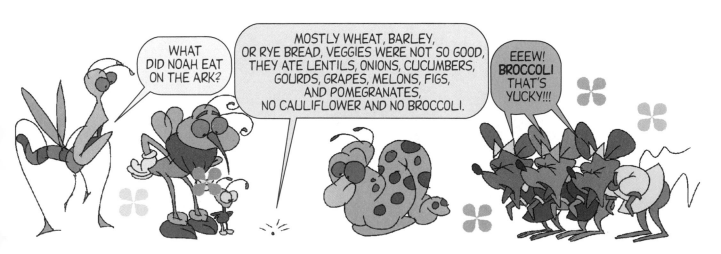

WHAT DID NOAH EAT ON THE ARK?

MOSTLY WHEAT, BARLEY, OR RYE BREAD, VEGGIES WERE NOT SO GOOD, THEY ATE LENTILS, ONIONS, CUCUMBERS, GOURDS, GRAPES, MELONS, FIGS, AND POMEGRANATES, NO CAULIFLOWER AND NO BROCCOLI.

EEEW! BROCCOLI THAT'S YUCKY!!!

Let's Make a Video about

BREATHE! DON'T FORGET TO **BREATHE!**

Your Family Video Theater

Mr. Noah's Family

Cast: Mr. Noah, Mrs. Noah, Ham, Shem, Japeth, Mrs. Ham, Mrs. Shem, Mrs. Japeth, Voice of God

Scene: Outdoors in front of ark

Narrator	The time came for Mr. Noah's family to come into the ark. Mr. Noah couldn't find Mrs. Noah.
Mr. Noah	What are you doing, hiding under the gangplank?
Mrs. Noah	So you found me. What do you want?
Mr. Noah	The Lord has told us to get on board.
Mrs. Noah	Oh, NO! ATICHOO!
Mr. Noah	What do you mean, "Oh, NO! ATICHOO"?
Mrs. Noah	Well, those animals—you know I'm allergic to cats—and I don't like snakes . . . or spiders . . . or . . .
Mr. Noah	Now, now, Mrs. Noah, come on now. You'll get used to it.
Mrs. Noah	I never thought God would shut me up in a zoo when he knows I'm afraid of wild animals.

HEY BARNEY, WHAT IS **GOPHER WOOD?**

NOBODY KNOWS FOR SURE.

THE ARK WAS PROBABLY NOT POINTED AT BOTH ENDS LIKE A SAILBOAT.

YOU CAN FIT MORE ANIMALS INTO A "BOXY" BARGE THAN YOU CAN FIT INTO A "POINTY" SAILBOAT.

HOW CAN SO MANY SMARTS FIT INTO SUCH AN ITTY-BITTY BRAIN?

Mr. Noah	Mrs. Noah, would you rather stay out here and drown?
Mrs. Noah	No, I wouldn't, but O dear, O dear . . . ATICHOO! And what about those mosquitoes I saw flying on board? You know they always make a meal of me!
Mr. Noah	God will help us do his will. You'll see.
Mrs. Noah	I'm frightened. His will scares me.
Mr. Noah	It's more scary *not* to do it, Mrs. Noah.
Mrs. Noah	I'm coming. I'm coming . . . ATICHOO! O dear, O dear . . . ATICHOO! Sometimes it's so hard, dear God, but your will is best. Help me to do what you want me to do.
Narrator	When Mr. Noah's family was all safely inside, God shut the door, and the rain rained and rained and rained.

Indoor scene—on board the ark.

Mrs. Noah	What's the matter, Ham?
Ham	Oh, dear! You know I get claustrophobia (that's a big word for not liking being shut into a small space). If only we could leave the door open!
Mrs. Noah	Now, now, Ham. You'll get used to it. God will help us. Just think, your father didn't even pass the woodworking class at school, but God helped him build the ark.
Ham	You're right, Mother. You're right.
Mr. Noah	Well, now, Mrs. Noah, it's time to feed the animals. The children will help me. Don't panic. We have enough food to keep the animals satisfied and God is keeping them calm with each other. Why don't you make us some vegetable sandwiches?
Mrs. Noah	Now, I can do that!

Japheth	Father, remember that we're going to have a baby!
Mr. Noah	Yes, I remember. How could I forget? I'm not sure how we can take care of a new mother and baby.
Japheth	It will be all right, Father. We can make a bed out of one of the animal troughs and line it with hay.
Mrs. Noah	But we don't have a doctor on board.
Mr. Noah	God will show us what to do.
Shem	I feel sick.
Mrs. Noah	Oh, dear, oh dear! We forgot about his motion sickness. We didn't bring any pills with us.
Mr. Noah	We'll all get used to it. You see, at night the boat will gently rock us to sleep.
Mrs. Ham	I hate peeling potatoes. Why can't Mrs. Japheth do them?
Mrs. Japheth	Why should I? I'm going to have a baby.
Mrs. Shem	Don't look at me!
Mr. Noah	Now listen, everyone. We are the only people left on earth. Eight of us—saved from the flood by a loving and merciful God. Here we are arguing among ourselves already. We are behaving just like the people who were drowned. This must not be.
Shem *Ham* *Japheth* *(together)*	We're sorry! (*All hug and shake hands.*)

Mrs. Noah	I think this is a good time to pray together.
All	Good idea. I agree. (*All kneel in a circle.*)
Narrator	So God helped Mr. and Mrs. Noah and their children, Shem, Ham, and Japheth, and their wives, to learn to live together and work together and pray together. They lived in the ark for one year and ten days. Then God let them out of the ark. The sun gloriously broke through the clouds. They looked up in the sky and saw a rainbow across the sky, and then they heard God speak.
Voice of God	Never again will I destroy all living things as I have done this time. I am putting my rainbow in the clouds. It will be the sign of my promises to the world.
Shem	Listen! I think I can hear the rainbow singing.
Narrator	Sure enough, the rainbow was singing a beautiful promise song. Mr. Noah and his family thought it was a beautiful song, and they all worshiped God. This is the way the song went.

Rainbow Song

Words and Music by
JILL BRISCOE and LARRY MOORE

Moderately

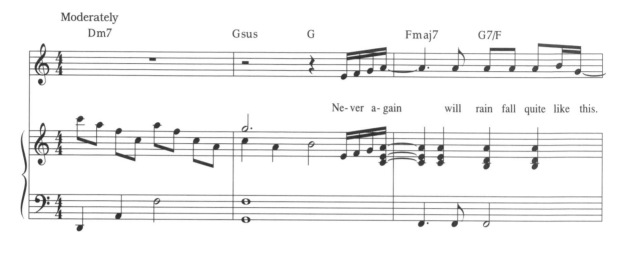

Ne-ver a-gain will rain fall quite like this.

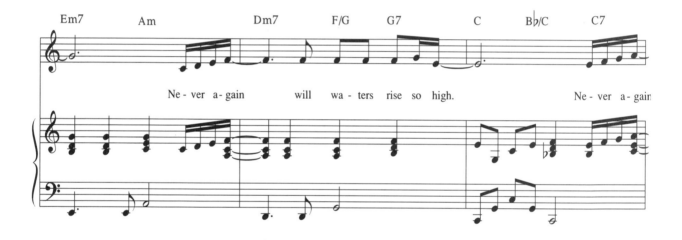

Ne-ver a-gain will wa-ters rise so high. Ne-ver a-gain

will floods de-stroy all life. Ne-ver a-gain will men so fear the

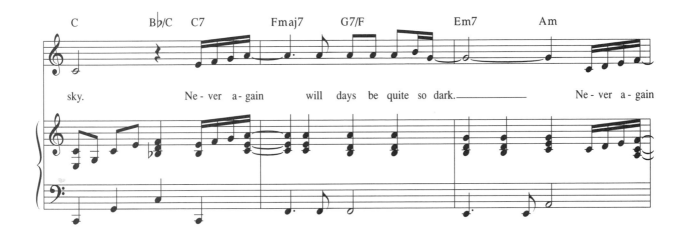

sky.   Ne - ver a - gain   will days be quite so dark._____ _____   Ne - ver a - gain

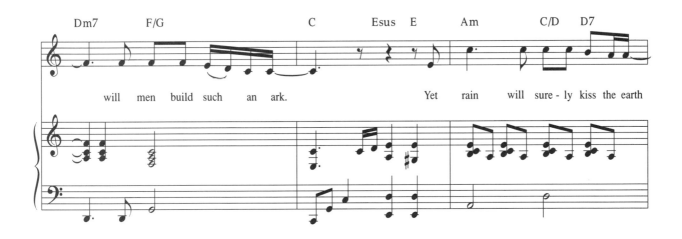

will men build such an ark.   Yet rain   will sure - ly kiss the earth

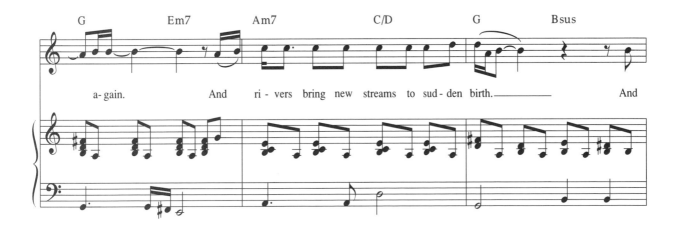

a- gain.   And   ri - vers bring new streams to sud - den birth._____ _____   And

o-ceans will crash up-on the san - dy shores. And ice and snow soon melt a-gain to

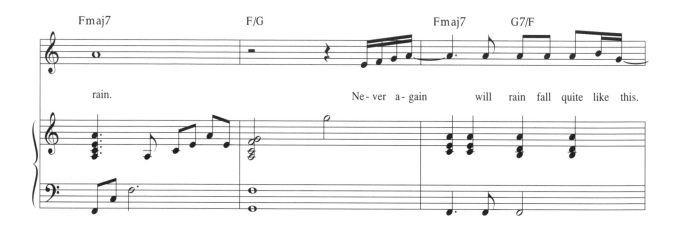

rain. Ne- ver a- gain will rain fall quite like this.

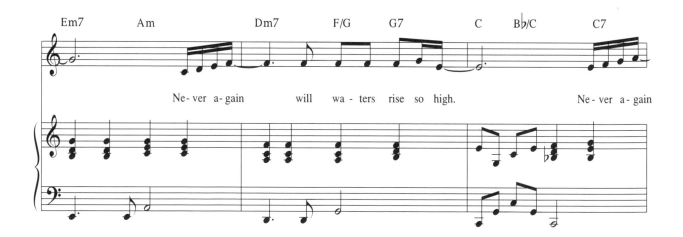

Ne- ver a- gain will wa- ters rise so high. Ne- ver a- gain

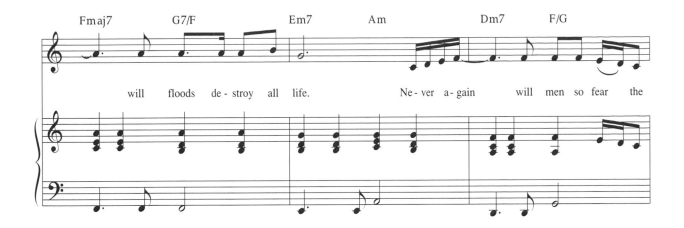

will floods de - stroy all life. Ne - ver a - gain will men so fear the

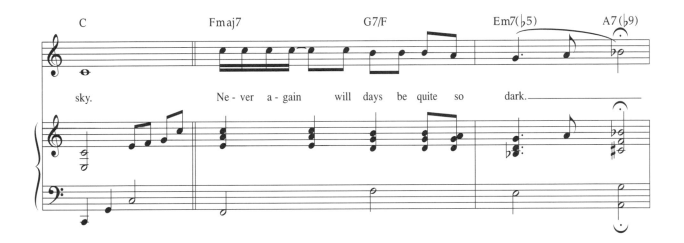

sky. Ne - ver a - gain will days be quite so dark.

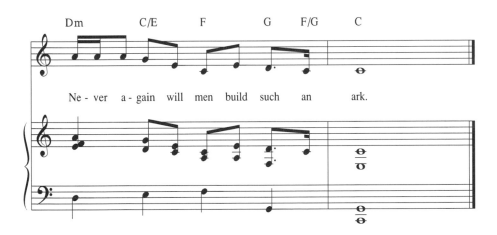

Ne - ver a - gain will men build such an ark.

ABRAM

Ur was a very nice place to live. The houses were modern for those days, the climate was pleasant, and the people were friendly. Abram lived in Ur with his wife, Sarai. In fact, the whole family lived there: Abram's father, Terah, and his brothers Nahor and Haran. Haran died quite young, so Abram and Sarai looked after Haran's son whose name was Lot. The people of Ur did not know about the Lord. They thought that there were some gods who sailed across the sky in the new moon when it looked like a boat, so they worshiped the moon once a month. But Abram believed in the Lord. We don't know if somebody told him about the Lord, if he found out on his own, or if God had a special way to teach him.

One day the Lord said a very strange thing to Abram. "I want you to leave Ur and all your friends and go somewhere else."

"Where do you want me to go, Lord?" Abram asked.

"I'll tell you when you get there," was the Lord's answer. This was very unusual, but the Lord wanted Abram to trust him, which Abram did. He and Sarai and Terah and Lot gathered together all their possessions and servants and headed out in the direction that the Lord had said.

One of the main reasons that Abram was prepared to leave his nice home was that the Lord had promised to bless him and bless many nations through him. There was no way that Abram understood all this, but he believed what the Lord said and wanted to find out what it all meant.

The journey took quite a long time because the animals that carried the family and their belong-

How does God talk to me?

ings, and any other animals and maybe servants, had to walk. There weren't any big trucks in those days. When the animals saw some nice grass they stopped to eat it, and when they came to some water they stopped for a drink. After days of traveling, they arrived in Haran, where they stayed for a while. There Terah died. He was very old, 205 years old, to be exact. The Lord then said to Abram, "It's time to move on, Abram. Go southwest, young man." Abram was only seventy-five years old at the time.

When Abram and his family and all his animals arrived in the place that the Lord had led them to, Abram was happy. He built some altars in different places and worshiped the Lord. He thanked God for being good to him.

But something was puzzling Abram. The Lord kept reminding Abram that many people all over the world would be blessed through him. Abram knew that this didn't mean just through him personally, but through his children. The problem was he had no children, even though his name meant "exalted father." He and Sarai talked about it and they thought they would solve the problem by doing something that the Lord did not have in mind—having Abram take a second wife. A son was born whose name was Ishmael. The Lord explained to Abram that he and Sarai would

have a son, and that through this son great blessing would come to people all over the world. The Lord said that there would be so many blessed people that they would be as many as the grains of sand on the shore and the stars in the heavens. (God was using exaggerated language to show he meant many, many.) Abram knew what God meant and believed what the Lord had said.

Years later Sarai, who was an old lady by this time and whom God had renamed Sarah, had a son. She named him Isaac, which means "laughter," because she and Abraham were so happy. She could hardly believe what had happened. But God had said he would cause her and Abraham (the Lord by this time had changed his name to Abraham, which means "father of many") to have a son, and he had done what he said.

There were some problems between Isaac and his older half-brother, Ishmael, and this made Abraham unhappy. The only solution was for Ishmael and Hager, his mother, to go to live in the desert. God took care of them there just as he promised he would.

Abraham is such a wonderful example of what it means to believe in the Lord and to trust him in all things that Abraham is called the father of all believers.

Let's Pretend

CAMPING IN CANAAN

Abram walked into a sports store in downtown Haran. The shelves were packed with tents and camping goods, traps for catching quail (a bird that tastes something like chicken), bows and arrows, and toys.

The store belonged to a man named Jacob who smiled a big smile when he saw Abram coming into his shop. He knew Abram was a very rich man.

"Shalom, Abram," he said.

"Shalom, Jacob," Abram replied.

"What can I do for you?" asked the shopkeeper.

"I need a big tent, Jacob. But it has to be light as well as large, because I'll pick up and move around a lot."

Jacob was worried. "I hope you aren't moving back to Ur, sir. We would miss you here in town."

"Not to Ur, Jacob, not back to Ur."

"Maybe," Jacob asked hopefully, "the tent is for a vacation?"

"We aren't going on vacation," answered Abram. "We're moving south toward Canaan. Somewhere new to start a family."

"Canaan?" spluttered Jacob. "Why . . . why . . . or I should ask *where* are you headed for? I have heard it's very dangerous along that route."

"I don't know where we will end up," said Abram quietly, "but we are going."

Jacob stood there with his mouth wide open. At last he found his voice. "How big a tent do you want, sir? Will your mother, sisters, and brothers, and all your family be going along with you? And what will you do there?"

"The tent I want is just for my own family. My relatives will all stay behind, except my nephew Lot and his

67

family. He will come along. We'll try a little shepherding to tide us over until we get settled."

"Excuse me for saying so, sir. Are you sure this is the right thing to do?"

"God will take care of us," Abram replied. "This was his idea, in fact."

Jacob picked a large tent and had his helpers pack it up for Abram. Jacob couldn't wait to tell his wife all about this.

Meanwhile, Abram was wondering how to tell *his* wife all about this. The beautiful Sarai met him at the door of their elegant house. They lived in a mansion, with smooth stone floors and heaters for the cold winters, in the best part of town. Sarai loved every bit of it, not to mention the green, watered garden looked after by dozens of servants.

She was glad to see Abram. They loved each other very much. Life was extra good, except for one thing. They had no children. One day, Sarai hoped, the Lord would bless them with a son, and she would decorate one of the huge rooms in the mansion in baby blue.

"Sarai," Abram said, "we are moving."

"Moving!" exclaimed Sarai. "Where? And when? And . . . Abram, why?"

"Because the Lord God has come to me and told me to take you and leave this place."

"But . . . but . . . where are we going? Back to Ur of the Chaldeans? Really, Abram, I thought we would stay here forever. It was

such work to pack up all our things, not to mention all the things of the people who work for us, and come here to live."

"We won't be going back to Ur, Sarai," Abram explained. "The Lord God hasn't told me yet where we are going. He's just told us to pack up and head south, and he'll tell us when we get to the right place. We'll start out toward Canaan."

"Canaan!" Sarai whispered in horror. "That's no-man's land! And where will I hang my chandelier? From the tent pole?" she demanded, her voice rising. "And where will we tell the moving van to go to if we have no new address?"

Abram talked quietly about life in a tent, being shepherds, moving around to where they could find grass, starting a family in a new place. He tried to make it sound exciting, like a camping vacation, but both of them knew it was all going to be very, very difficult indeed.

So Abram and Sarai packed up all of their things that would fit into a big tent and sold the rest of their goods. Their friends and relatives warned them: "You could get yourselves killed. Or starve to death."

But Abram would not change his mind. "God will care for us and bless us. He has promised," was all Abram would say. Then, taking Lot and his family, their servants and their animals, they said good-bye to all their friends and left Haran forever.

ABRAHAM & ME

Can you imagine how hard it would be to sell everything you have—your house, cars, toys, and most of your clothes—and live in a tent in a desert far from the kinds of towns or villages we have for the rest of your life? You would have sand in your sandwiches and no ice cream. Never would you go to McDonald's again. Have you ever moved to another city? It's hard, isn't it? It would be especially hard if you didn't even know where you were going to end up.

Sarai must have worried about having a baby in the desert too. Abraham and Lot must have worried about the cattle thieves and robbers with no police to protect their families and their possessions. But Abraham trusted God and set off not knowing where God was leading him. The most important thing in his life was to obey God. That was even more important to Abraham than his elegant mansion and all his wealth. The hard thing was to do what God said without being told

what would happen next. But Abraham believed that since God couldn't tell a lie he would keep his promise to look after them and carry them every step of the way.

Sometimes people promise us things and then they don't keep their promises. We feel really let down and wonder if we can trust them again. But we will never feel let down by God, because even though we may wait a long, long time, God's promises *never* fail.

How can we know what God promises? How did Abraham know? We are not sure if Abraham just knew by God putting his messages in Abraham's mind or if Abraham heard a real voice.

We have something Abraham did not have: God's promises written down in the Bible. They tell us God will do what is best for us because he loves us forever. See if you can find some of those promises in your Bible, and then thank God for keeping them.

Look in 1 John 1:9, Psalm 31:23, Matthew 28:20, Psalm 62:8.

Somedays you want to go out to play but when you look out the window you see it is raining. Are you disappointed? Maybe you don't like the rain because it spoils your fun, but we would be in big trouble without the rain. Have you ever taken a walk in the rain with your parents?

- Rain makes food grow in our fields.

- Rain cleans up everything.

- Rain gives us water to drink.

Abraham would have to hunt for water for all his animals because it didn't rain very much where he was going. Ishmael and Isaac wouldn't have too many rainy days when they couldn't play outside.

Abram believed the Lord.
Genesis 15:6

Fancy Footnotes

WEEEEEEEE! WE'RE ON VACATION

OH, NO! I FORGOT TO PACK THE UMBRELLA, THE PHONE, THE HAMMOCK, AND THE MAYONNAISE.

WE WON'T NEED THEM.

With such a big family, what do you think they had to spend for food or other things they needed. Did they use dollar bills like ours? No, they used a funny sort of money. They used *things* to buy *things*. If they wanted a cooking pot, maybe they used an animal skin to buy it. If we used things to buy things and you wanted a new video game, maybe you could use your new football to buy it. Does that sound like it would be a lot of fun?

Have you ever been outside and heard a siren and seen the police car's flashing lights as it raced along the road? Perhaps the officers are rushing to stop a crime. When Abraham moved there were no cars or police officers. If crime happened, Abraham himself and his male servants would arm themselves and fight. They didn't have guns either. What weapon do you think they used?

OH, NO! I FORGOT TO PUT OUT THE CAT.

HOW LONG WILL WE BE GONE?

OH, ABOUT 40 YEARS.

How did Abraham get to work? "Early in the morning Abraham got up and saddled his donkey" and took off (Genesis 22:3). Before camels came into widespread use, travelers used donkeys to make long trips.

Who worked for Abraham? Abraham did a lot of big business and had 318 trained men working for him. Every week Abraham traveled and did business with people he met. Instead of leaving Monday morning on a plane or in a car or bus, he took all his family and animals with him. Think of all that luggage! There were no motels then. Just imagine your father doing that.

What do you think they ate at lunch? Maybe some dates, figs, grapes, or some bread cakes, nuts, olives, pomegranates—maybe a lamb chop or two?

73

SMILE!

PARTICIPANTS ARE ENCOURAGED TO EXPAND AND IMPROVISE, USING THIS MATERIAL AS A GUIDE. ALLOW YOUR IMAGINATION TO "PEEK AROUND THE CORNER OF THE VERSE" AND SEE WHO IS COMING.

SMILE!

Let's Make a Video about

Your Family Video Theater

Grandpa Abraham's Story

Cast: A very old Abraham, Isaac, and Isaac's twelve-year-old twin sons, Esau and Jacob.

Scene: Traveling along a path.

Jacob	How much longer until we arrive at Grandpa Abraham's tent?
Isaac	When the sun sets over the western hills we should be there.
Esau	Will we have time to go hunting when we get there?
Isaac	No, it will be almost dark!
Esau	I want to go hunting tomorrow morning.
Jacob	I don't want to go hunting. I don't like killing things.
Esau	That's because you're a big baby!
Isaac	Now, boys, that's enough of that kind of talk.
Esau	Well, he is a big baby. He just stays at home helping Mother.

THIS IS AN EGGHEAD. IT KNOWS A LOT OF STUFF.

ISAAC MEANS LAUGHTER.

ABRAM MEANS EXALTED FATHER.

WHEN SARAH WAS 75 YEARS OLD, SHE WAS SO BEEEEUTIFUL, A KING WANTED TO MARRY HER!

LISTEN, DEARIE, SHE GAVE BIRTH TO ISAAC WHEN SHE WAS 90 YEARS OLD!

Isaac	I said, "That's enough!" If that is what he likes to do, that doesn't mean he's a baby. Now let's change the subject.
Jacob	I hope Grandpa will tell us a story.
Esau	I hope he'll take us hunting!
Isaac	I'm afraid his hunting days are over. He's an old man now.
Jacob	But he's not too old to tell us a story.
Esau	I don't want to listen to a story. I want to go hunting.
Isaac	I know a story that you will like to hear, Esau. It's about when I was your age.
Esau	Is it exciting?
Isaac	Just you wait and see!

Later that evening outside Abraham's tent.

Esau	Grandpa! Dad says you are too old to go hunting but you know some good stories.
Abraham	Well, it's true that I can't get around like I used to, but I'll be glad to tell you a story.
Jacob	Tell us the one about Dad when he was our age.
Abraham	Are you sure you want me to tell them that one, Isaac?
Isaac	Yes. It's time they knew about what God did in my life.
Abraham	One day the Lord told me to take your father with me to Mount Moriah. He was just a boy at the time.
Esau	When can I climb Mount Moriah, Dad? There'll be great hunting up there, I'm sure.
Jacob	Can't you think about anything but hunting? Go on, Grandpa.
Abraham	So early the next morning we got ready and set off on a three-day journey.
Esau	Did you have to hunt for food on the way, Grandpa?
Abraham	I'm sure we did but I don't remember any details. I had a lot on my mind.
Jacob	Like what, Grandpa? What were you thinking about?
Abraham	Your father had asked me why we had brought everything except the animal for a sacrifice to the Lord.
Isaac	I remember asking you about that as we climbed the mountain.

Abraham	Do you remember my answer?
Isaac	I could never forget. You said, "God will provide."
Esau	Well, what's so unusual about that?
Abraham	You'll see in a minute.
Jacob	So what happened when you got to the top of the mountain, Grandpa?
Abraham	Your father and I built an altar, laid the wood on it, and then . . . (*Abraham's voice trails away into silence and he looks into the flames of the campfire.*)
Esau	Then what, Grandpa? Go on! What happened?
Abraham	I took your father, tied him up, and . . .
Jacob	Were you playing a game with him, Grandpa?
Abraham	It was no game, Jacob. It was deadly serious.
Esau	You mean you were tying him up because he had been bad and needed punishing?
Abraham	No, he'd been a good boy. He wasn't being punished.
Jacob	Well, why did you tie him up? What were you doing?
Abraham	I was going to offer him as the sacrifice. I was . . .
Esau and Jacob (together)	Grandpa! You don't mean it.
Abraham	Yes, boys, I do mean it. But let me explain.
Jacob	I don't want to hear any more of this story.
Esau	Oh, you're a baby. Go on, Grandpa, I want to hear the rest.
Abraham	Don't worry, Jacob. It all worked out fine. Your father is alive and well, as you can see.
Jacob	Why would you do such a thing?
Abraham	Because the Lord had told me to do it.
Esau	But why did he do that?
Abraham	He wanted to see if my faith was strong enough to believe that everything would be all right.
Isaac	Boys, you need to understand something I've never told you before. Grandpa is a very special man. God has chosen him to be the father of a great number of people: grandchildren like you and your children and their children. And many, many

	thousands of people who would be blessed because of Grandpa.
Esau	What does this have to do with you being tied up and offered as a sacrifice?
Isaac	Well, I'm special too. You see, Grandpa had no children. When he and Grandma were old, I was born in a special way.
Abraham	And if your father did not live, there would be no possibility of God's promise working out. Your father was the only hope.
Jacob	Grandpa, what were you thinking while all this was going on?
Abraham	I was thinking Isaac must live and even if he dies, God will raise Isaac up again.
Esau	Wow! I would never have thought of that. So what happened?
Abraham	Just as I was ready to do what God had said, there was a loud voice telling me not to harm your father.
Isaac	I was so relieved. Then I said to Grandpa, "Look over there. There's a ram caught by its horn in a thorn bush."
Abraham	So I untied your father and we rushed over and sacrificed the ram.
Isaac	Then I remembered what Grandpa had said on the way up the mountain, "The Lord will provide."
Abraham	I knew God would but I must admit I didn't know how he would do it.
Isaac	We didn't stay long on the mountain. It was getting late and we had a long way to go home.
Abraham	Right. But we built an altar to the Lord before we left, and we called it "Jehovah Jireh."
Jacob	I know what that means. "God will provide."
Abraham	That's right, and don't ever forget that lesson.
Esau	But it was a hard thing that God asked you to do. If he had a son, would he ask the son to die?
Abraham	I'm sure he would.

Tell Me, Mr. Abraham

Words and Music by
STUART BRISCOE and LARRY MOORE

MOSES

Hundreds of years after Isaac's son Jacob and Jacob's famous ruler-son Joseph had lived in Egypt, the new Pharaoh (Egyptian kings were called pharaohs) was cruel. All the Hebrew people (Israelites) who lived in his land were slaves. Pharaoh had them whipped and had all the baby boys that were being born murdered. Among the Hebrews, God's people, was a mother named Jochebed and a father named Amran who had a little girl Miriam and a little boy Aaron age three. When the Pharaoh decided to kill the newborn babies, Jochebed and Amran were very worried because Jochebed had just given birth to a beautiful little baby boy. She and her husband couldn't bear to let the soldiers take him, so they hid him for three months. If you have a baby brother or sister you'll know how hard that must have been. Babies make such a noisy noise when they are hungry.

When the baby was three months old, Jochebed knew she couldn't hide him any longer, so she put him in a floating basket among the reeds on the Nile River. She knew this was the place Pharaoh's daughter always came down to bathe. When the princess came to the river she heard the baby crying and sent one of her servants to get the little boat-basket out of the reeds. The princess was sorry for the baby and realized he must belong to a Hebrew family who was trying to hide him. Miriam, the baby's sister, was watching to see what would happen. She ran up to Pharaoh's daughter and asked her, "Shall I get a Hebrew mommy to feed and care for the baby for you?"

"Yes," Pharaoh's daughter answered, "and I will pay her for it." Guess what Miriam did. She ran home and brought back her own mommy. "Take care of this child for

me, and I will give you your wages," said the princess to Jochebed. Imagine how happy Jochebed was to take her own baby back home safe and sound? She was able to have him all to herself until he was old enough to be taken to the palace to be brought up and educated as a king's grandson. Then the princess took him home and called him Moses.

One day years later, when Moses was grown up, he lost his temper trying to stop an Egyptian who was beating a Hebrew slave. Moses was drawn into the fight and killed the Egyptian. Pharaoh heard about it and was really angry. So he sent soldiers to kill Moses. Moses had to run a long way into the wilderness to hide. In fact, he became a shepherd and spent many years there looking after sheep. Moses would take the sheep he cared for into the wilderness to try to find something for them to eat. He would look for little patches of grass under the prickly scrub bushes that grew in the sand. Sometimes the sun was so hot the brittle little bushes would catch fire and burn up.

After Moses had been a shepherd for forty years, God came and spoke to Moses in a very strange way. One day Moses noticed a little bush burning that looked quite different. It was burning, but it didn't burn up. Moses had never seen anything quite like this before, so he stopped to see what it was all about.

He saw an angel in the bush and heard God's voice. God wanted Moses to go back to Egypt to rescue all the thousands of Hebrews who were still slaves to Pharoah. The Hebrew people were going to be freed from the cruel king in Egypt. God would bring the Hebrews safely out of the country and Moses would be their leader. Moses didn't want to go at first but he decided to obey. After God had sent all sorts of trouble (plagues) to the Egyptians, they let the people leave. The Hebrews traveled toward a piece of land named Canaan. God had promised Abraham long ago that Canaan would be given to the Hebrew people.

God was with his people after Moses brought them out of Egypt and God did wonderful miracles. He made a dry path for them to cross through a sea and sent them special bread from heaven to eat. Except for a very few of them, the people forgot to say thank you and be grateful. Instead of traveling across the wilderness for just a few months and arriving in the wonderful country God had promised to them, the people grumbled and groused and wouldn't do what God told Moses to tell them to do even though they knew they should. So God had them spend forty years wandering around in the wilderness. Only a handful of the people who escaped from Egypt went into Canaan—the Promised Land. Two men, Caleb and Joshua, led into Canaan all the children who had been born and grown up in the years they had lived in the wilderness.

Even Moses died in the wilderness and never went into Canaan. But God took him to a very high mountain and let him see that fine land he wanted the Hebrews to live in.

Moses was one of the greatest leaders who ever lived anywhere in the whole world, a special man chosen by God to do a special work.

THIS IS A STORY TOLD AS FANTASY MARRIED TO FACT TO BE MIXED WITH FAITH AND LAUGHTER, LOVE AND JOOOOOY.

Let's Pretend

ON THE TRAIL TO THE PROMISED LAND

Benjamin and Jacob trudged along with their families. It was hard walking the trail made more dusty by hundreds of feet that had gone before them. Their legs ached, and the hot sun gave them each a headache.

"Wasn't it exciting when the Lord stopped the waters from drowning us!" said Benjamin, trying to get his mind off things.

"Yes," agreed Jacob, "what a miracle! And then when we were safely across to the other side the waters came rushing back and covered the Egyptian army that was trying to catch us. That was neat."

"I haven't been able to sleep very well," Benjamin said. "I've been waking up thinking the soldiers are still chasing us."

"I've been scared to go to sleep because of all the scorpions," Jacob admitted, feeling a little ashamed. After all, he was the oldest boy in his family and felt he shouldn't be afraid of creepy, crawly bugs.

"We didn't have any scorpions in Egypt," Benjamin grumbled.

"Or so little water," Jacob added, catching Benjamin's attitude.

"Do you think we'll get to the Promised Land today?" asked Benjamin.

"I don't think so. My dad said it could be three months before we get there," answered Jacob.

"Three months!" Benjamin exclaimed. "You mean we have to walk in this awful sand in the hot sun for three months?"

I GO; MILT NOW AND MILT WHAT YOU SAY. I WILL TEACH YOU WHAT YOU SHALL SAY. Exodus 4:12

83

"Well, I don't know," Jacob answered. "Only the Lord knows how long it will take us."

"I'm so thirsty," murmured Benjamin. "But my mother told me there's not a lot of water left in the water skins. She was grumbling about it too. She wonders if we should have come out here at the beginning of the dry season. I think she's scared."

"And my uncle was grumbling about the food," Jacob added. "When others start grumbling it's sort of catching like measles."

"I don't think God likes to hear us grumbling," said Benjamin. "I wouldn't if I were he. Just think—he did all those miracles to get us out of Egypt."

The boys found out they felt a lot better when they thought about the exciting things God had done for them instead of grumbling about the sand and heat and scorpions. It helped them to stop thinking about the empty water skins too.

"I'm surprised you're frightened of scorpions, Jacob," Benjamin teased. "Just think of all the thousands of bugs we left behind in Egypt."

"Well, they were in the Egyptians' houses, not ours," Jacob answered. "And even though they were so many, they were harmless fleas or grasshoppers. I'll never forget going into houses on an errand for my dad and seeing servants shoveling dead frogs out of their master's house. Ugh!"

"And what about the way the Lord sent that terrible thunderstorm and the lightning and hailstorm!" Benjamin said.

"That was awesome!" Jacob interrupted. "Leah and Joel found some hailstones as big as my fist." Jacob clenched his fist to show just how big he meant.

Suddenly the people ahead slowed their walk, and the boys found themselves in a crowd of grownups gathering around Moses. They were all grumbling. Some didn't like the wild food they were finding along the way. Others were angry about the hot sun and having to carry all their bedding and pots and dishes with them. Some mothers were griping about the tents they slept in at night.

"When we were back in Egypt at least we had proper houses to live in and meat to eat," one woman complained to her neighbor.

"To say nothing of juicy fruit," the other replied.

Benjamin and Jacob felt very uncomfortable. Moses' face looked very serious indeed. The boys glanced at each other.

"God has told me that he has heard your grumbling. You saw how he sweetened for you the bitter water at Mara. Now he will send you bread from heaven to eat in the morning and he will send you meat in the evening," he added. "You know, you're not grumbling against me but against God. He is not pleased with your ungrateful hearts. He wants you to

be thankful and remember all the wonderful things he has done for you."

The next morning when Jacob and Benjamin got up they saw that the ground was covered with thin white flakes. It looked like frost.

"It's the bread from heaven God promised to send," Moses told the people. They called it manna.

The boys collected the manna every day for their families. Their moms made it into sweet-tasting cakes or boiled it like cereal.

In the evening the Lord sent quails so the people had meat to eat.

Benjamin and Jacob learned to say grace before every meal. They knew that the Lord was looking after them and didn't want them to be ungrateful or grumble anymore. God saw the way the boys tried to be thankful and God was pleased with them. He decided one day Benjamin and Jacob would go into the Promised Land.

MOSES & ME

God gave Moses lots of plans and rules for the Israelites to follow so they could live together in a safe, healthy, and loving way. Moses wrote down what God told him, but the most important rules were written by God himself on flat pieces of stone he gave to Moses on Mount Sinai: the Ten Commandments. We still use the Ten Commandments today.

You can read the Ten Commandments in the Bible in Exodus 20, but here are

GOD'S TEN RULES FOR BOYS AND GIRLS

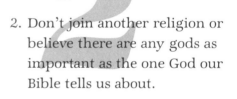

1. Love God more than anything else you own or anyone you know. Love everyone else more than yourself. Always put others first.

2. Don't join another religion or believe there are any gods as important as the one God our Bible tells us about.

3. Don't swear. That's the same as calling God names.

4. Make sure the Sabbath or Sunday is a special day, the one when you go to church and worship God with his other children. Have a rest. Make it a day different from the other days of the week.

86

5. Respect your mother and father by obeying them. Think nice things about them and say nice things to them.

6. You are not allowed to kill another person however mad they make you feel.

7. When you grow up and get married, stay married to each other and have sex only with the person you marry.

8. If someone owns something you must never take it without asking. If they say no, you can't have it.

9. Don't ever lie. Always tell the truth, even if that gets you into trouble. Don't tell tales or pretend someone has done something wrong when they haven't, however much you want them to get into trouble.

10. Don't let yourself want what you don't have when someone else has it. Instead, be glad about what you *do* have.

STUFF Near stuff Nea

The tabernacle was a tent church that had three parts surrounded by a curtain fence.

The **outer court** had a big entrance so people could bring in their animals to be sacrificed. There was an altar in the outer court and a big basin or bowl of water so priests could wash themselves before doing their work.

The tabernacle had an **inner court** which contained a golden candlestick, or lamp, with seven branches. The candlestick burned oil all the time. There was also a table with twelve loaves of bread, and also an altar of incense (a very expensive perfume).

The inner court had a **special inside room** that was separated by a thick curtain. In this special room, called the Holy of Holies, was the ark of the covenant (a small box or chest covered with gold). There

Bronze laver or basin
(Outer Court)

Brazen Altar
(Outer Court)

Outer Court

were two carved cherubim (something like an angel) on the cover. The cover had a name: "The Mercy Seat." Inside the box were the tables of stone with the commandments God gave Moses on Sinai, a bowl of manna, and Aaron's rod. Only the high priest could go into this room and he could go in only once a year.

The **high priest** wore special clothes too. Did you know he had bells on the bottom of one of his garments? He also wore white linen shorts, a white tunic woven all in one piece, a sash, an ephod (or apron) embroidered in blue, purple, gold, and red, a breastplate of jewels, a golden band on his forehead and a cone-shaped hat.

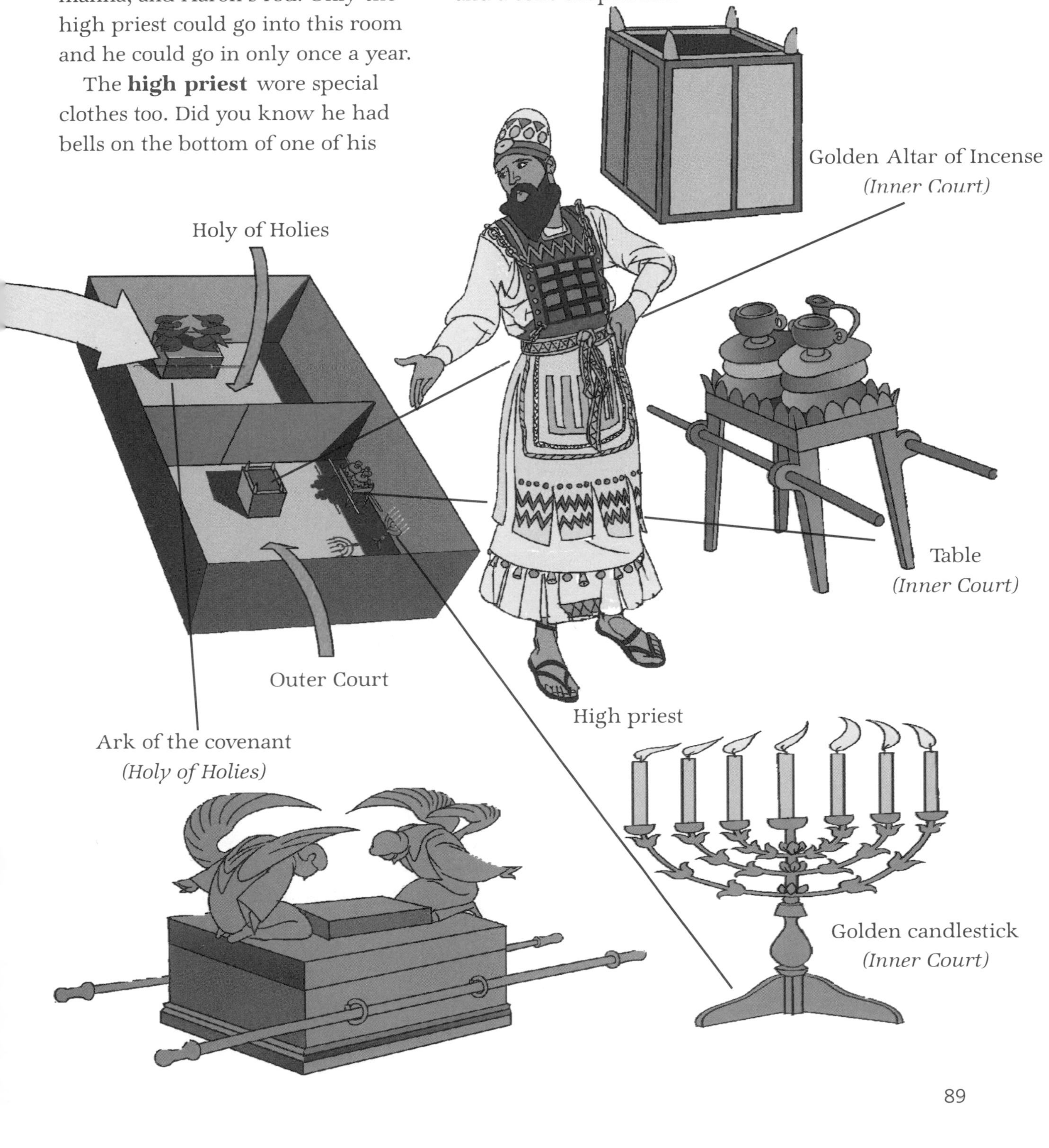

Golden Altar of Incense
(Inner Court)

Holy of Holies

Table
(Inner Court)

Outer Court

High priest

Ark of the covenant
(Holy of Holies)

Golden candlestick
(Inner Court)

89

stuf

The trip from Egypt to the Land of Canaan should have taken the Israelites only a couple of months, even if the people walked slowly and rested many times.

The trip took the Israelites forty years. They wandered and wandered all the time. Imagine living in a desert or wilderness for a week. Imagine living there for over two thousand weeks?

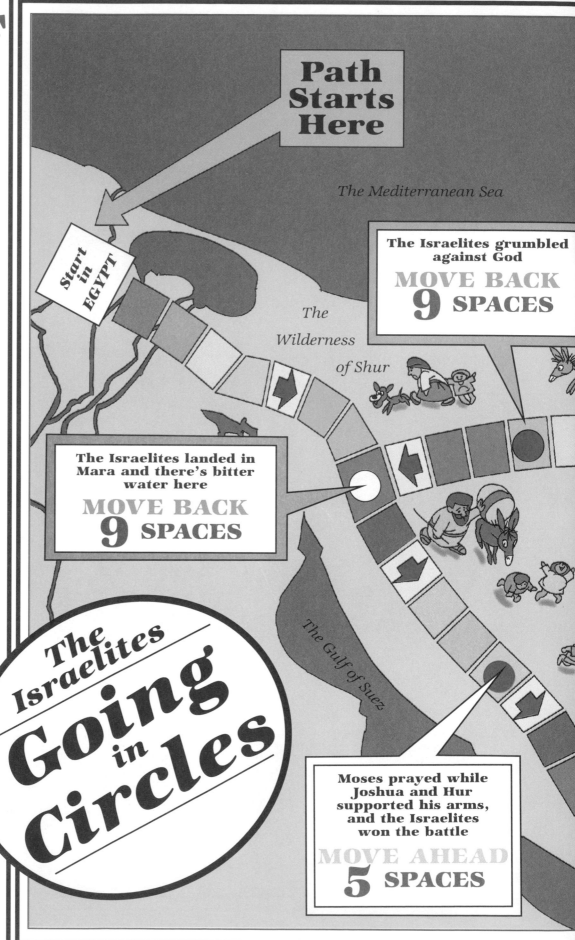

Path Starts Here

Start in EGYPT

The Mediterranean Sea

The Wilderness of Shur

The Israelites grumbled against God
MOVE BACK **9** SPACES

The Israelites landed in Mara and there's bitter water here
MOVE BACK **9** SPACES

The Gulf of Suez

The Israelites Going in Circles

Moses prayed while Joshua and Hur supported his arms, and the Israelites won the battle
MOVE AHEAD **5** SPACES

Path Ends Here

The Land of Canaan

The Israelites didn't believe God

GO ONE MORE TIME AROUND THE BOARD

The Israelites disobeyed God

MOVE BACK 6 SPACES

The Sinai Desert

The Gulf of Agabar

The Ten Commandments were given here

MOVE AHEAD 3 SPACES

The Red Sea

Joshua and Caleb believed God, so...

GO STRAIGHT INTO THE LAND OF CANAAN

Use your fingers to do some desert wandering. Stop at some of the spots the Israelites visited. You can probably make the trip in less than four minutes.

Play a game with this map by tossing a penny into the air. If it lands with the tail up, go forward four spaces with another penny. If it lands with the head up, go forward three spaces.

OWW! THIS THING POKED ME IN THE EYE.

Let's Make a Video about

Your Family Video Theater

Caleb and the Cloud

Moses

Cast: Father, Caleb, Rebecca, Mother, two or three children.

Scene: Campground at twilight.

Narrator   God wanted his people to know he was with them to protect and help them when they left Egypt. God cannot be seen as people can be seen, but when he led his people to safety they could see the very air around God was on fire. There was smoke, too, which made a billowy, brilliant, and beautiful cloud. The fire at night and cloud in the day covered the tabernacle after it was built.

God told his people that whenever the cloud stopped they were to stop. Whenever it moved on they were to follow it. Sometimes the cloud moved on at the wildest times. It wasn't convenient, the people thought, and they would grumble about it. But still they wanted to stay close to the visible presence of God.

Father   Caleb, come and help me get the tent up.

Caleb   All right, Father, but I'm so tired. We've been walking all day in the hot sun, and I had to carry some of Rebecca's things at the end.

Fancy Footnotes

A PHARAOH IS A KING WITH A POINTY HAT.

YEAH, BUT A REAL KING WEARS A CROWN.

THE PARTING OF THE RED SEA WAS LIKE THIS. EXCEPT FOR THE WOOD FRAME OF COURSE.

WHATEVER YA DO, DON'T KICK THESE BOARDS.

YA MEAN DON'T KICK THIS BOARD?

Father	The men have already put up the tabernacle. Now we can put up our tents around it so it will be in the middle of our camp. Look! The cloud of God's glory has come to rest over the Holy of Holies. That means we can rest here a few days.
Caleb	All right! I love to see the cloud. When it comes down on the tabernacle I know God is with us. And when it stops we can play for a while and you can tell stories and we can eat our supper.
Father	Hurry now, Caleb. It's getting dark and your mother is fixing that supper you love.
Narrator	While Caleb and his father set up the tent, Mother and Rebecca gather some sticks for a fire on which to cook the supper of quail meat and manna cakes. The family sits on the ground in front of the tent to eat. But as the sun sets it gets chilly and they go inside to make their beds on thick mats with woolen blankets.
Mother	Caleb, it's time for bed. Bring your sisters and brother in now and we will say our prayers.
Narrator	Caleb and Rebecca stretch their tired bodies beneath the cozy blankets while Mother hums a lullaby and Father begins to cover the tent door.
Father	Oh, no!
Mother and children	What's the matter? What's wrong?
Father	The cloud is moving.
Mother	It can't be. We're nearly settled in bed for the night. The children are exhausted.

Rebecca	What does it mean?
Caleb	Father, we are all so tired, and I hate to travel by night, even though the cloud becomes a fire and lights the way.
Mother	But we must follow the cloud, Caleb. God is in the cloud. We must stay near him. It would be a disaster if we lost sight of him. (*Children grumble and complain.*)
Father	Silence, all of you. We must go where the cloud goes.
Mother	Come on, up you go. Let's make a game of it. Caleb, help your father with the tent.
Father	No, Caleb, go to where the donkeys are and get Old Reliable. Rebecca, you go along in case he's stubborn. The rest of us will take care of the tent.
Caleb	Yes, Father. Come on, Rebecca. We'd better hurry.
Rebecca	Everybody in camp looks worried and people are talking so loudly tonight. Usually at night it is quiet but not tonight. It's really noisy here. I don't like to travel at night, it's so-o-o dark.
Caleb	The fire cloud makes it light. And the moon is almost full tonight. Oh, boy, everyone's looking for their donkeys. Do you see Reliable?
Rebecca	There he is, with his nose into something.
Caleb	You hold the rope while I pull up the stake. Uhhh! Come on, Reliable. COME ON! Get your nose out of that stuff. He found some scroungy plant by this rock. Pull the rope hard, Rebecca. Get your nose out of there, Reliable. RELIABLE!!
Rebecca	Push his head up, Caleb.

	Everybody is leaving. I can't pull any harder. *(shouts)* Come on, Reliable!
Caleb	Keep pulling. I'll whack his rump. *(shouts and whacks)* Go, go, go!! GO! GO! RELIABLE! *(sighs)* I don't know what's wrong with him.
Rebecca	Please, Reliable, move!
Caleb	He's moving. Good boy, Reliable.
Narrator	The family is ready to load up Old Reliable. Then each one picks up a bundle. The camp leaders get the people ready to march. Slowly the cloud lifts and begins to move. Caleb chuckles quietly to himself.
Caleb	I think it's funny! Even though we are all so sleepy. It's . . . it's sort of an adventure.
Mother	Father, what will we do if we don't get enough rest?
Father	There are more important things than sleep, Mother. The blessing of the children lies in the obedience of the parents! To stay where we are and lose sight of the Lord would be the end of us. God is teaching us a lesson.
Mother	Come, children. Let's be first in line and cheerful. Let's follow God with *all* our hearts!
Narrator	So Caleb and his family learned to be obedient the hard way. It is not always easy to follow the Lord but there is no other way to stay happy in life. When Caleb grew up he still followed the Lord with all his heart. He remembered being a little boy and keeping God's glory cloud in sight. He had decided to follow God and stay close to him and do whatever God told him to do. He knew that was the most important thing in the whole wide world. God was so pleased with Caleb that he let Caleb enter the Promised Land.

Following the first five books of the Old Testament are the twelve historical books. Their names are:

Joshua
Judges
Ruth
1, 2 Samuel
1, 2 Chronicles
1, 2 Kings
Ezra
Nehemiah
Esther

These twelve books tell the story of the Israelites and how God dealt with them as they lived in the land of Canaan.

The first historical book, Book of Joshua, tells about the struggles the Israelites had entering the land. Joshua was one of the twelve spies sent by Moses into the land of Canaan. Moses knew Joshua was as wise as he was fearless and often Joshua helped Moses. God told Moses to train Joshua to be the next leader who would take the Israelites into Canaan, the promised land. The Canaanites who lived there were wicked people. God said they had to be removed, but that was not easy to do. Joshua was a good leader and while he lived, the people obeyed God. Just before Joshua died, he

THE BOOKS OF HISTO

asked people to choose between worshiping idols or serving the living God. They all promised to serve God. But when Joshua died, the Israelites did not do what God commanded, there were all kinds of problems.

Samuel was one of the great leaders after Joshua died and his story is in Book 2. After Samuel, the Israelites were ruled by kings. Saul, David, and Solomon were three great kings. Their stories are also in *David Drops a Giant Problem: And Other Fearless Heroes*, Book 2 of the series, Baker Interactive Books for Lively Education.

JOSHUA

Moses was a very important man. He was also very busy, for he was in charge of all the Israelites he had led out of Egypt. There may have been over two million people and they had many problems. One young man named Joshua was helpful to Moses, and Moses liked him a lot. He became Moses' personal helper.

The Israelites were living in a very unpleasant wilderness. There were lots of rocks and snakes and plenty of sand and not much else. The Israelites did not like living in the wilderness. They were on their way to a much nicer place—Canaan—that God had promised to give them to live in (which is why it was called the Promised Land). But many other people already lived there, and naturally they did not want Moses and his people coming to live with them. The people of Canaan were cruel and did many evil things. God had told Moses it was all right to take over their land. Nobody was very happy about this arrangement. Getting into Canaan was going to be difficult, but no one knew how difficult.

Moses sent twelve men into the Promised Land to have a look around to see what the Israelites should expect. Joshua and Caleb were two of them. The spies had to be very careful how they talked to people and how they dressed and how they asked questions. If the people of Canaan guessed they were spies, the men would be killed.

In Canaan there were cities with high walls all around, too high to climb, and the only way in was through big gates. The spies planned to slip into the city and hope nobody noticed they were Israelites.

Once inside, the men looked around to learn all they could about the people who lived there. How many people were there? How many weapons did they have? How high were the walls? How strong were the gates? When the spies had learned all they could in the cities, they went into the country. There they wanted to learn about how hilly it was. If there were rivers, how deep and wide were they? Did the farmers live in villages? If so, how many were there? The Israelites needed to know all these things so that they could get ready to come into the land and take it over as the Lord had promised.

One day the spies had a real scare. They saw some giants, big men who looked very fierce. Spying was dangerous work.

The twelve men also saw that the land would be a good place to live, to keep animals, and also to grow crops of grain and fruit. Moses had told the spies to bring some fruit back with them. The Israelites had been a long time without fresh fruit in the wilderness and they heard that the fruit in the Promised Land was very good. They were right. Joshua and his friends found a bunch of grapes so big that they had to tie it on a pole and two of the men carried it.

The spies went back into the wilderness and told Moses and the people what they had seen. Joshua and Caleb said everything would be fine, because the Lord would be with them and that it was a very good land. But the rest of the men said the giants were too big and they were scared to go ahead. The people did not believe Joshua and Caleb and became afraid also. Moses believed the two and said they should go ahead into the Promised Land. The people became so angry they wanted to kill Joshua and Caleb. But Joshua and Caleb trusted the Lord and continued to be very brave.

Because the people did not trust the Lord they refused to go into Canaan and chose instead to go back into the wilderness. There weren't any giants in the wilderness, but there weren't any giant grapes either! The Israelites stayed there for forty years. Then one day the Lord said that it was time for Moses to go to heaven. Moses made Joshua the new leader of the Israelites.

After many difficulties, Joshua got all the people into the Promised Land. There were some hard battles but the Lord was with his people. Joshua taught them to obey the Lord and kept reminding them that the Lord was on their side.

Joshua was a good man who loved and served the Lord.

Let's Pretend

THIS IS A STORY TOLD AS FANTASY MARRIED TO FACT TO BE MIXED WITH FAITH AND LAUGHTER, LOVE, AND JOY.

HELLO! ANYBODY IN THERE?

THE RED CORD

Tobi was eight years old. He lived with his father in a small city called Jericho. Tobi's mother had died when he was small, so he had never known her. But he had a favorite aunt named Rahab. She was a kind lady, and when his father had to go away Tobi would go to stay with Rahab. She lived in a house that was built into the city wall. People traveling through Jericho could stay there overnight. Aunt Rahab was a good cook, and tired travelers knew they could get a good meal and a night's rest at her house.

Tobi liked to climb the palm trees that grew in Jericho. He would scramble up the trunk of a tree, and when he got to the top

he would hold on with one hand and with the other he would pick the sweet sticky dates. The travelers enjoyed the sweet dates that Tobi picked for them.

One day just as the city gates were being closed two young men came to Aunt Rahab's house and asked if they could stay overnight. They were strangers in the town; nobody had ever seen them. They had no donkeys and spoke with an accent different from the people of Jericho. Aunt Rahab said that her house was full, but they could sleep on the flat roof under the starry sky if they wanted to. They were happy to hear that. After they had eaten a big meal finished off with some cool, clear water from one of Jericho's famous springs and some of Tobi's dates, they climbed up onto the roof and unrolled their sleeping mats.

Tobi sometimes slept on the roof when it was very hot because the roof was the coolest place. The two men did not see him lying on his mat in the corner. They began to talk very quietly. Tobi heard what they were saying and realized they were spies sent by Joshua, the leader of the Israelites who were

BE STRONG...BE WITH YOU WHEREVER YOU GO. FOR THE LORD YOUR GOD WILL BE

Joshua 1:9

101

camped in the wilderness. Tobi hoped the men would not discover him. But a fly settled on his nose, and he gave a loud sneeze.

The men rushed over to where Tobi was lying and said, "So you were spying on us, were you?" They looked very fierce.

"No, sirs," he replied, "I wasn't spying on you, but I heard that you are spying on us. We have heard about Joshua and his people and how the Lord has looked after you. My Aunt Rahab is a believer in the Lord, and I am too."

Aunt Rahab heard the talking up on the roof and came to ask the men to be quiet. But when she heard Tobi's story, she said to the men, "You are most welcome in the name of the Lord. We know that he is the one true God."

Just then there was a commotion in the street below, a loud knocking on the door, and cries of "Open up in the name of the king of Jericho. We know you are hiding spies in the house." Quickly Aunt Rahab hid the men under some flax that was drying on the roof. She rushed downstairs.

"There are no spies here," she said. That was a lie, but she believed that it was better to tell a lie than to let the men be killed. "Some men who were here left at dusk! If you hurry you may catch them." The men believed her and went away. Then the city gates were closed. "

You must run away to the hills and hide until they give up looking for you," said Aunt Rahab to the two men. "But when you come back and take the city please help my family and me to escape." The men promised to help.

"I'll show you the way," said Tobi, and before Aunt Rahab could object, he scram-bled over the side of the house on the outer part of the city wall and down a date tree, with the two Israelites after him.

Tobi led the men to the safety of the hills. "Don't forget that Aunt Rahab said you must stay here for three days until the king's men stop looking for you. Then it will be safe to go back to your camp," he told them.

"Thank you, Tobi, for helping us," the men said. "We won't forget to help you when the army returns. Nothing will happen to you or any of Aunt Rahab's family."

"But what if something happens to you? How will the other soldiers know who we are?" Tobi asked. "We need something to mark us out."

The spies smiled at each other and said, "Tobi is a smart kid! He's right. We need to have something to put in the window of Aunt Rahab's house so that we can tell the soldiers to rescue the people who live there." But they couldn't think of anything.

Tobi had an idea. One of the men wore a red cord around his forehead. It made him look very brave and fierce, but it was meant to keep the sweat out of his eyes. "Give me your red cord," he said. "I'll hang it in the window on the wall." The men agreed, and Tobi went home again, carrying the red cord and being careful not to let the city gate guards see him climb back up the date tree.

So the red cord was placed in the window. When Joshua's army came, the city walls collapsed, except for one small part. Aunt Rahab's house was not damaged and the red cord was hanging from the window. The two spies saw it and rushed to bring out Rahab and her relatives. They all escaped safely. The Israelite soldiers were destroying everything and setting the city on fire. Then someone said, "Where's Tobi? Did we forget him?"

"I see him," said one of the spies. "He's climbing back up the date tree by the city wall."

Everybody watched the young boy disappear inside the house. Then he appeared at the window, untied the red cord, and scrambled quickly down again before running as fast as he could back to the family. "I couldn't leave the red cord," he grinned. The family all gathered around and patted their young hero on the head. "Oh, I almost forgot," he added. "I brought you some sweet, sticky dates." Everybody laughed and hurried away to safety.

Joshua & Me

Are you ever frightened? Sometimes your teacher may ask you to do something hard and you don't think you can do it. Or a new family moves in next door and you are scared to invite the new children to play. Or you may be learning a new sport and don't think you can hit the ball or do it right. Joshua was scared when God gave him something new and difficult to do but God told him not to be scared. God gave Joshua some special promises: God would give Joshua strength and courage to do his work. God would always be with Joshua. Did you know that God gives you the same promises?

Have you ever gone to a new school, moved to a new house, met new friends, had a new adventure? Well, Joshua led over a million people into a new land. About that many people live in the whole state of Maine. Imagine all of them moving down to Florida. That would be a real adventure!

How do you get across a river? wade? swim? skip from one stone to the next? use a bridge? One day the people of God had to carry the ark of the covenant through a deep river. There was no bridge so God parted the water and let the people cross over on dry ground. How's that for a miracle? That ark was about forty years old and had been carried to many places. It always traveled first, ahead of the people. This was to show the people that God was leading them through the wilderness and God knew the way. The people understood it was safe to follow God.

Joshua chose twelve men, one from each tribe, to carry twelve big stones from the river they had just crossed to build a monument. Can you describe what a monument looks like? What is it made of? The monument Joshua and the men were building was to remind the children of Israel how God stopped the waters of the Jordan River so the people could cross on dry land.

THERE'S NOBODY IN HERE!.

YA MEAN IT'S SAFE TO COME IN HERE?

YEAH. HE MUST'A SEEN ME COMIN' AN' JUMPED CLEAN OUT'A HIS BOOTS!

The trumpets carried by the priests who marched around the walls of Jericho were made of the horns of wild goats or rams. They were called *shofars*. Because only two notes could be played on these horns and the sound could be heard for a long distance, the horns were used to give battle signals.

Let's Make a Video about

PARTICIPANTS ARE ENCOURAGED TO EXPAND AND IMPROVISE, USING THIS MATERIAL AS A GUIDE. ALLOW YOUR IMAGINATION TO "PEEK AROUND THE CORNER OF THE VERSE" AND SEE WHO IS COMING.

I CAN'T STAND IT ANY MORE! I THINK I'M GOING BUGGY

Your Family Video Theater

Twelve Stones

Joshua

Cast: Mother Naomi and daughter Tabitha

Scene: A field outside Gilgal near the Jordan River

Tabitha	What a lovely day. I'm glad we came for a picnic.
Naomi	The air is so fresh and the breeze is cool.
Tabitha	Look at that beautiful butterfly. I wish I were a butterfly.
Naomi	Why ever would you want to be a butterfly?
Tabitha	If I were a butterfly I would flutter by!
Naomi	*(laughing)* You're a silly little pumpkin. Come, help me get the food ready.
Tabitha	What are we having to eat today? Not barley loaves and fishes, I hope.
Naomi	'Fraid so, Tabitha. But I have some juicy figs too.
Tabitha	I wish I were a juicy fig.
Naomi	Oh no. Why would you want to be a juicy fig?
Tabitha	Then I would dance a fruity jig.
Naomi	Wherever did you learn to talk like that?

HOW YOU GONNA MOVE THIS HUNK O' LEATHER?

WE'RE GONNA DO IT LIKE THE EGYPTIANS DID IT,

BUT WE'LL USE DRINKING STRAWS.

SLIDE THE STRAWS UNDER THE BOOT.

HEY! THESE AIN'T GRAPES THEY'RE... RATTLESNAKE EGGS!

Tabitha	From my friend Ruth. She does it all the time.
Naomi	Does she do it at school?
Tabitha	Oh, yes. She changes all the boys' names into girls' names. She calls Seth Boaz, Beth Soaz, and Danny Finehas, Fanny Dinehas.
Naomi	She shouldn't do that.
Tabitha	Why not? They're only boys.
Naomi	Now Tabitha. That's not nery vice. *(laughing)* Now look what you've done. You've started me talking like you! I mean that's not very nice.
Tabitha	Come on. Let's go for a walk. I want to climb that hill and see what's on top.
Naomi	Great! I'll race you to the top.
Tabitha	Oh, that was a great race. I nearly beat you. When I'm a little older I will beat you every time we race. But now I'm out of breath. I must lie down and be quiet for a few minutes.
Naomi	That will be nice. Nery vice! Oops, there I go again.
Tabitha	What are those big stones standing in a circle? How did they get there?
Naomi	They were put there many years ago by Joshua and his men when they crossed over the river down there in the valley.
Tabitha	But they are so big. Where did they get them from?
Naomi	They came out of the river.
Tabitha	They just came out of the river on their own?
Naomi	No. The men carried them out. Joshua told them to do it.
Tabitha	Why would he tell them to do that?

108

Naomi	Well, it was like this. When our ancestors wanted to cross the Jordan River into the Promised Land, the river was flooded. So the Lord told Joshua to instruct the priests to carry the ark of the covenant into the middle of the river.
Tabitha	Did they do it? Did they just walk out into the river carrying the ark?
Naomi	They certainly did.
Tabitha	I think that was crazy. They could have drowned, and the ark could have been washed away.
Naomi	That's true. But the Lord had promised to hold back the water while the priests stood in the middle of the river.
Tabitha	And did he do it?
Naomi	Of course he did. The Lord always keeps his promises.
Tabitha	Then what happened?
Naomi	All the people of Israel went across the river with dry feet.
Tabitha	When did the river roll back again?
Naomi	After the priests had left and the men had picked out the twelve stones.
Tabitha	But what was the point of the stones?
Naomi	So that when mothers like me bring children like you for picnics, the children will see the stones and ask about them. Then the mothers can talk about the wonderful things the Lord has done.
Tabitha	They are a kind of reminder, aren't they?
Naomi	That's right, and we need reminders, because we forget things so quickly.
Tabitha	Thanks for telling me this. It was a streat gory. I mean great story. But why are there twelve stones?
Naomi	One for treach ibe. I mean each tribe. Each of the twelve tribes of Israel.

I WAS JUST **KIDDIN'** 'BOUT THE

CHOMP, CHOMPSLURP CHOMP.

NOW, **PUSH!**

These innovative books will appeal to parents who want to teach biblical truths to their children in a fresh and exciting way. The interactive presentation of Bible stories, using songs, drama, and cartoons, makes the **B.I.B.L.E.** books ideal for family devotions. Kids will actually look forward to spending time together learning about God's word. No more coaxing and cajoling.

This multi-media approach can add excitement and enrichment to other educational settings:

- Home school
- Christian school
- Children's church
- Sunday school

Songs and readings from these books are also available on audio.

Six adventures are waiting in each book of the **B.I.B.L.E.** series. Take an excursion with your family from creation through the New Testament. Look below at characters and events found in all four books:

$14.99 each • Hardback • 112 pages

Available now:

Moses Takes a Road Trip
And Other Famous Journeys

- *Creation*
- *Adam and Eve*
- *Noah*
- *Abram*
- *Moses*
- *Joshua*

ISBN 0-8010-4183-X

Jesus Makes a Major Comeback
And Other Amazing Feats

- *John the Baptist*
- *Jesus' Birth*
- *Jesus' Miracles*
- *Jesus' Big Week*
- *Jesus' Resurrection*
- *Luke*

ISBN 0-8010-4197-X

Coming in 1997:

David Drops a Giant Problem
And Other Fearless Heroes

- *Samuel*
- *David*
- *Solomon*
- *Jeremiah*
- *Daniel*
- *Jonah*

ISBN 0-8010-4216-X

Paul Hits the Beach
And Other Wild Adventures

- *Peter*
- *Paul's Life*
- *Paul's Journeys*
- *Timothy*
- *James*
- *John*

ISBN 0-8010-4202-X

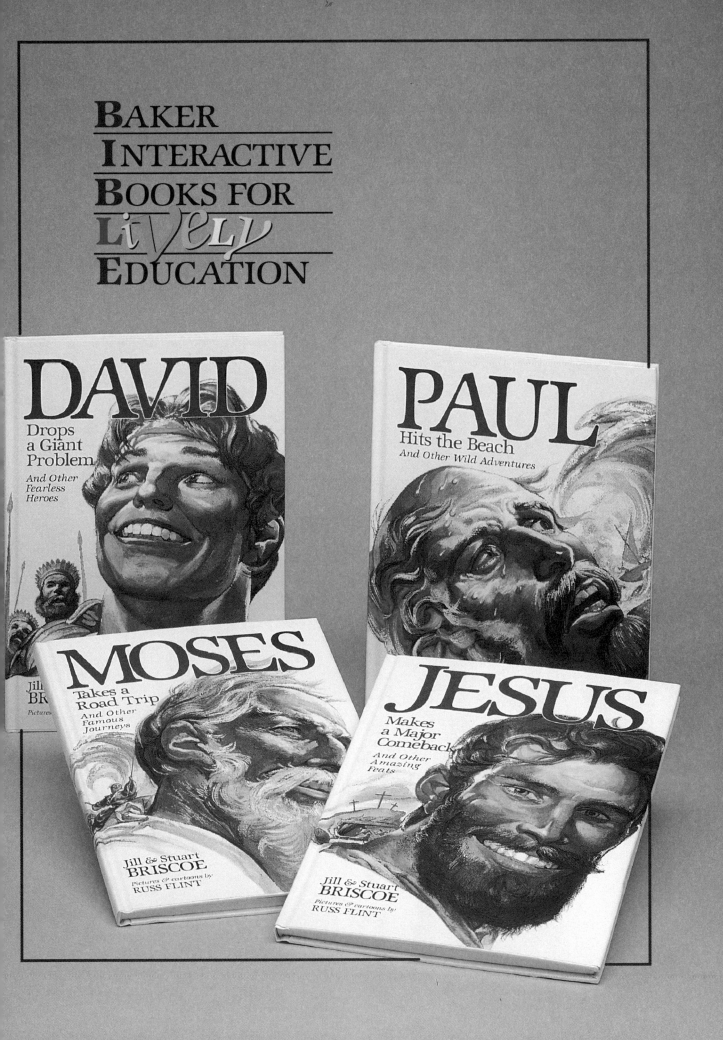

BAKER INTERACTIVE BOOKS FOR LiVELY EDUCATION

DAVID Drops a Giant Problem
And Other Fearless Heroes

PAUL Hits the Beach
And Other Wild Adventures

MOSES Takes a Road Trip
And Other Famous Journeys

Jill & Stuart BRISCOE
Pictures & cartoons by RUSS FLINT

JESUS Makes a Major Comeback
And Other Amazing Feats

Jill & Stuart BRISCOE
Pictures & cartoons by RUSS FLINT

Jill and **Stuart Briscoe** are the parents of three grown children and the grandparents of nine. Jill has written more than forty books, and Stuart more than fifty. Stuart serves as senior pastor of Elmbrook Church in Brookfield, Wisconsin. Jill is an advisor to women's ministries at the church, and director of Telling the Truth media and ministries. Both are worldwide speakers at retreats and conferences. The Briscoes live in Oconomowoc, Wisconsin.

Russ Flint is the designer/illustrator of many children's books, including *Let's Make a Memory*, *Let's Hide a Word*, *My Very First Bible*, and *Teach Me About Jesus*. He regularly contributes artwork to such magazines as *Ideals* and *Guideposts for Kids* and is co-founder of Dayspring Card Company. He has also illustrated such familiar classics as *Legend of Sleepy Hollow*, *A Christmas Carol*, *Swan Lake*, and *Little Women*. He lives in Greenville, California.